A Start W

Dipl.-Ing. Juergen Pintaske

17 July 2018

1 Charles Moore - Forth - The Early Years: Background information about the beginnings of this Computer Language

2 Charles Moore - Programming A Problem Oriented Language: Forth - how the internals work **Now as eBook and as print book (e/P)**

3 Leo Brodie - Starting Forth, the classic

4 Leo Wong / Juergen Pintaske / Stephen Pelc FORTH LITE TUTORIAL: Code tested with MPE VFX Forth, SwiftForth and Gforth

5 Juergen Pintaske – A START WITH FORTH – Article Collection – 12 Words to start, then 35 Words, Javascript Forth, much more **(e/P)**

6 Stephen Pelc - Programming Forth: Version July 2016

7 Tim Hentlass - Real Time Forth

8 Brad Rodriguez - Moving Forth / TTL CPU / B.Y.O. Assembler

9 Chen-Hanson Ting - Footsteps In An Empty Valley issue 3

10 Chen-Hanson Ting - Zen and the Forth Language: EFORTH for the MSP430G2552 from Texas Instruments

11 Chen-Hanson Ting - eForth and Zen - 3rd Edition 2017: with 32-bit 86eForth v5.2 for Visual Studio 2015

12 Chen-Hanson Ting - eForth Overview

13 Chen-Hanson Ting - FIG-Forth Manual and Test on FPGA 1802

14 Chen-Hanson Ting - EP32 RISC Processor IP: Description and Implementation into FPGA – ASIC tested by NASA

15 Chen-Hanson Ting – Irriducible Complexity

16 Burkhard Kainka - Learning Programming with MyCo: Learning Programming easily – PC independent (Forth code to follow soon)

17 Burkhard Kainka - BBC Micro:bit: Tests Tricks Secrets Code, Additional MicroBit information when running the Mecrisp Package

18 Burkhard Kainka&Thomas Baum – Sparrow Programs, TINY13

Contents

Download parts of the book for print at

https://wiki.forth-ev.de/doku.php/en:projects:a-start-with-forth:start0

Link to the Forth Bookshelf:

https://www.amazon.co.uk/Juergen-Pintaske/e/B00N8HVEZM

File: A_Start_With_Forth_eBook_v18b21.docx

1 – Introduction

A different view of the Programming World

And before the question comes up: it is Bites not Bytes – the little bites of Forth collected here.

Forth has been around for many years – supposedly 2018 there will be a special event celebrating 50 YEARS OF FORTH, and hopefully the inventor Charles Moore will be participating.

There is a wide range of information available on the Internet about Forth. Too much information and unfortunately very unstructured.

I faced the same problem, when I came back to learning a bit more about Forth after 30 years. Over the years, I had flicked through the Starting Forth by Leo Brodie book I had been given by a customer as a Thank You for the good technical support with the CDP1802 processor.

When I looked around, there was a lot of information around, mostly for more experienced people in programming than I am.

Knowing MPE and Stephen Pelc at the time helped, but I could not find the documentation and hardware descriptions to be able to digest it in very small bites for my level of knowledge.

Over the last 4 years I got more into it, got to know many more people in the Forth community who helped.

In this book, I want to collect the material I used for the software and hardware aspects and on the different platforms.

Infection Area – There is a danger that you might like the concepts shown here – independent of other languages you use privately or in your work. Forth has a way to make you think about problem solving.

Risk of Addiction – It seems that the way Forth works fits the "brain setup" of some people very well – reflecting how they work anyway. And there is the other group – they detest it. But it is probably like Marmite, very polarizing.

Brain Massaging – Forth probably adds another way of solving problems – and this applies to ANY problem – independent of but including software.

Problem Solving – The very structured way, starting with very small bits and extending them into Words (as they are called), basically: defining new words, merging then into phrases, chapters and finally the book is ready (your required solution of the specified problem).

Testing – as Forth is interactive and even the compiling only takes seconds – often less – you stay very close to your problem without interruption, can try out options quickly, test them until ready and document this part – sorry, no chance to go for lunch while the compiler takes over. In this area Forth works best and fastest from my understanding compared to other languages.

Mixed Language Programming – MPE has introduced a product called Sockpuppet, where the MPE VFX Forth is linked to other languages – at the moment mostly C – and all the testing advantages are accessible then via the Forth Add-On. Both language groups can work independently in their best area of knowledge.

Forth Bookshelf – Over the last 4 years I got to know many people in the Forth community, and some agreed to have their documents being stored somewhere formatted and published as eBook first and then later probably as print if there is interest. As eBook publication, the information exposed to a wider audience by amazon worldwide, not just to the inner circle.

No Hardware - to get a very general understanding of Forth, the investment is just this eBook – the examples can run on probably on any PC – and some parts as well on tablet and smartphones – then using Gforth. The relevant links for download are shown in this eBook.

On Controllers – As hardware person, I want to see LEDs flash, make sounds and drive RC-Servos - here the TI MSP430 is used and as well an ST ARM board. Some documentation here, more in Part 2.

I must thank the many people that helped to make this book and the bookshelf possible and happen, and here just a few names:

Charles Moore, Stephen Pelc, Leon Wagner, Michael Kalus, Paul Bennett, Dirk Bruehl, Matthias Koch, Ulrich Hoffmann, Chen-Hanson Ting, Tim Hentlass, Leo Wong, Duncan Louttit, Steve Teal, Ralf Lieb, and the Forth-ev.de Website, where many news could be published.

Juergen Pintaske, ExMark, June 2017

My thanks go to the people who allowed me to use their material in this eBook, especially Nick Morgan/Twitter; Stephen Pelc/MPE; Dirk Bruehl/Bruehlconsult; Michael Kalus, Matthias Koch, Frank Sergeant, Vic Plichota and Paul Bennett, HIDECS.

Important Note: This eBook is for Starting Forth. It only touches the basics of this extensible language. A next step would be to look at the Forth LITE Tutorial for more explanations, and deeper details in Stephen Pelc's book for example, for the more experienced programmers. A link to the Forth Standard is given in the Appendix. Part 2 of A Start With Forth will go more into hardware. Feedback always welcome. Please to epldfpga@aol.com.

If you enjoyed this Book, please leave a comment at amazon.

2 – Facts from an Interview with Charles Moore

There is a very nice Interview of Chuck Moore in the book I saw, **Masterminds of Programming by Chromatic, Federico Biancuzzi** at https://www.safaribooksonline.com/library/view/masterminds-of-programming/9780596801670/

A few selected quotes from this interview describe Forth better than I could:

1 How do you define Forth?

Chuck: Forth is a computer language with minimal syntax. It features an explicit parameter stack that permits efficient subroutine calls. This leads to postfix expressions (operators follow their arguments) and encourages a highly factored style of programming with many short routines sharing parameters on the stack.

3 You consider Forth a language toolkit. I can understand that view, given its relatively simple syntax compared to other languages and the ability to build a vocabulary from smaller words. Am I missing anything else?

Chuck Moore: No, it's basically the fact that it's extremely factored. A Forth program consists of lots of small words, whereas a C program consists of a smaller number of larger words.

5 You don't have the C calling overhead.

Chuck: Right. This gives the programmer a huge amount of flexibility. If you come up with a clever factoring of a problem, you can not only do it efficiently, you can make it extraordinarily readable.

On the other hand, if you do it badly, you can end up with code that no one else can read—code your manager can't understand, if managers can understand anything. And you can create a real mess. So, it's a two-edged sword. You can do very well; you can do very badly.

6 What would you say (or what code would you show) to a developer who uses another programming language to make him interested in Forth?

Chuck: It is very hard to interest an experienced programmer in Forth. That's because he has invested in learning the tools for his language/operating system and has built a library appropriate for his applications. Telling him that Forth would be smaller, faster, and easier is not persuasive compared to having to recode everything. A novice programmer, or an engineer needing to write code, doesn't face that obstacle and is much more receptive—as might be the experienced programmer starting a new project with new constraints, as would be the case with my multicore chips.

14 Is this the source of the rumor that every time you ran across a new machine, you immediately started to port Forth to it?

Chuck: Yes. In fact, it was the easiest path to understanding how the machine worked, what its special features were based on how easy it was to implement the standard package of Forth words.

19 How do you define success in terms of your work?

Chuck: An elegant solution.

One doesn't write programs in Forth. Forth is the program. One adds words to construct a vocabulary that addresses the problem. It is obvious when the right words have been defined, for then you can interactively solve whatever aspect of the problem is relevant.

For example, I might define words that describe a circuit. I'll want to add that circuit to a chip, display the layout, verify the design rules, run a simulation. The words that do these things form the application. If they are well chosen and provide a compact, efficient toolset, then I've been successful.

24 What's the biggest mistake you've made with regard to design or programming? What did you learn from it?

Chuck: Some 20 years ago I wanted to develop a tool to design VLSI chips. I didn't have a Forth for my new PC, so I thought I'd try a different approach: machine language. Not assembler language, but actually typing the hex instructions.

I built up the code as I would in Forth, with many simple words that interacted hierarchically. It worked. I used it for 10 years. But it was difficult to maintain and document. Eventually I recoded it in Forth and it became smaller and simpler.

My conclusion was that Forth is more efficient than machine language. Partly because of its interactivity and partly because of its syntax. One nice aspect of Forth code is that numbers can be documented by the expression used to calculate them.

3 – A Collection of additional Aspects

Some Forth customers of FORTH, INC.
https://www.forth.com/resources/forth-apps/
and
https://www.forth.com/resources/who-uses-forth/
And see there as well the Evolution of Forth
https://www.forth.com/resources/forth-programming-language/

Some Forth customers of MPE Forth
http://www.mpeforth.com/about.htm

The widely-used Arduino Board is covered for example by AMFORTH and there is quite a bit of documentation:
http://amforth.sourceforge.net/

And there is noForth with many code examples
http://home.hccnet.nl/anij/nof/noforth.html

There are many more Forth implementations around that you can find on the Internet, I had to concentrate on a few here in this eBook.

And if there is a new chip but no Forth yet, the 3 Word Forth Interface in this eBook is a quick starting point:

Read from Memory Location
Write to Memory Location
Start a program on the new target chip

Using just these three commands implemented on the target chip, it is possible to work via a serial connection.
Using an existing Forth on a PC for example, all necessary words can then be implemented on the host.

4 - Start by Pretending to Invent a Language

Imagine to Invent a Language

As basis we will define virtually a piece of real hardware and will implement its functionality by just using the PC – replace all of the hardware necessary with Keyboard – PC – Screen. This first minimized version just uses the PW LED on the left of the ones shown. More will be used in the 35 Word Forth later on.

The real hardware consists of a few LEDs and a few Push-Button Switches. 1 LED PW on its own plus the 3 LEDs showing a switch status, 4 LEDs represent OUTPUTs, 4 LEDs for INPUT levels, and 4 LEDs more for Additional Functions; each "pin" can be either HIGH or LOW, 1 or 0 - and we end up with the header line for function (PW to A0) and a line for the relevant logic level. The 4 O, I and A values can be controlled as bits or nibbles, so you can as well count up and down later using the same display.

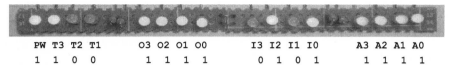

PW	T3	T2	T1		O3	O2	O1	O0		I3	I2	I1	I0		A3	A2	A1	A0
1	1	0	0		1	1	1	1		0	1	0	1		1	1	1	1

For now, we just want to set and reset this bit PW to 0 or 1. As a first programming exercise.

But describing how this should be programmed, is often more difficult than starting, thinking, designing and going through the process. So, let's get started and "imagine to define" a new computer language. At least the basics.

We want to have it done in a very simple way to be easily understood, so no difficult constructs in our language yet.

All normal ASCII characters can be used and are allowed to define our commands.

But we still have to separate these commands from each other, and we do it as in a normal writing – so a SPACE will do this. And from now on we call these commands WORDS as in normal writing and number them as we go through this process.

SPACE - word number 1 is as such the first word as just defined

Programming is one activity we have to do, but we have to make sure that we can add comments as well, explaining what the program does. So, a wall between the two areas is a good idea to divide program and explanations. The keyboard gives us for example two options \ and /. As dividing needs the / , the answer is clear: \ - the back slash will be used as indicator to tell the computer, that the rest of the line is for comments and ignored by the computer.

**SPACE ** - word 2 after SPACE

There are many aspects of programming we have to cover. For example, we have to set up a way to send ASCII characters to the display. Putting this text within 2 " quotes " would be a good way to define the text. And we have to define a command to send characters to the screen. We will just use in general the . (full stop) for this. And combined with the two quotes we know now already how to send the usual HELLO WORLD to the screen: ." HELLO WORLD " . Try it: enter . "HELLO WORLD " . But nothing happens yet. It is actually very clear why: the computer does not know that you have finished; entering ENTER / <cr> is used for this. Push the ENTER key after the ." HELLO WORLD " <cr> and do not forget the separating SPACE after the first ". Now the computer answers HELLO WORLD. We can do already what the other languages show off with. And the . on its own we deal with later.

SPACE \ ." xx " - now 5 words

It would nice, if we could define a way to combine what we know and call it something new. Like a paragraph we can relate to. We have to tell the computer though, how that

construct/"paragraph" starts and where it ends.
A : will start the new definition and a ; ends it.

SPACE \ **.** **."** xx **"** **:** **;** – **now 7 words**
Let us use the HELLO WORLD as an example. Let us define our first new word, give it the name
DISPLAYIT:
: DISPLAYIT ." HELLO WORLD " ; when we finish with the <cr> at the end, the
computer will answer OK, which means *understood*. If we enter now DISPLAYIT <cr> , the
HELLO WORLD appears on the screen. Enter the same DISPLAYIT, and another HELLO WORLD
is stuck onto the first one.
It would be nice if the new HELLO WORLD could appear underneath the first one. A word CR does
the job when we normally type, so we use it here as well as a new command.

SPACE \ **.** **."** xx **"** **:** **;** **CR** – **now 8 words**
We modify our : DISPLAYIT ." HELLO WORLD " ; to : DISPLAYITCR ." HELLO WORLD
" CR ; <cr> Job done. The computer answers OK, understood. And every time we enter
DISPLAYITCR <cr>, the same block is displayed, one underneath the other one now as we wanted.
An addition that would be nice is to be able to clean the display screen, and the word PAGE does
the job: all of the text that had been displayed before is deleted and we end up with a clean screen
page – nothing on it. Our cursor is at the top left position.

SPACE \ **.** **."** xx **"** **:** **;** **CR** **PAGE** – **now 9 words**
We have to pstore the current LED status of PW somewhere, and we have to be able to change it,
so we define **VARIABLEs** and store information there. We need 16 of them as we store a bit per
variable / LED for now. We use a new word **!** to store info into them and use @ to get the
contents back from a VARIABLE.

SPACE \ **.** **."** xx **"** **:** **;** **CR** **PAGE** **VARIABLE** **!** **@** – **now 12 words**, And these are all of
the Forth words needed for now to program our small example..

**And now let us put the words together, so we can control our virtual LED
PW. Type this code without the comments after having loaded
VFXTESTAPP.exe for example or another Forth. See** https://wiki.forth-
ev.de/doku.php/en:projects:a-start-with-forth:start

```
\ IMAGINE TO INVENT A LANGUAGE in 2 pages, do a small application v12  ExMark Nov2016
\ There are many comment lines for explanation – only the yellow ones are code.

\ We want to display these 2 lines on the screen and set these bits to 0 and 1. (Prepared already for later on).
\ PW only used
\ PW_T3_T2_T1 O3_O2_O1_O0 I3_I2_I1_I0 A3_A2_A1_A0 set XXh/l
\ 1 0 0 0  0 0 0 0  1 1 1 1  0 0 0 0
```

\ All of the Forth Words used and in the sequence as described above here:
\ **SPACE** \ . ." xx " : ; **CR** **PAGE** **VARIABLE** ! @

\ Define the text lines to display
: TEXT0 ." INVENT A LANGUAGE, do a samll application v4 ExMark Oct2016 " CR ;
: TEXT1 ." PW " CR ;
: TEXT2 ." 0 " CR ;

\ Define the variable PW needed for the LED to save the status in
VARIABLE PW

\ Define the 2 words to switch this 1 bit in the variable PW
\ to 1 (HIGH) and the word to set the variable to 0 (LOW)
: PWH   1 PW ! ;   \ set the variable PW to 1 (HIGH)
: PWL   0 PW ! ;   \ set the variable PW to 0 (LOW)

\ Define a word to display the contents of the variable as in TEXT2 and TEXT2

\ Define a word to display the variable:
: DISBIT PW @ . SPACE ;

\
: BITPW   DISBIT ;

\ And now to send the text line TEXT1 and the Variable value to the screen
: Display   CR TEXT1 DISBIT ;

\ **Use a new word MS**, which adds a delay in milliseconds before continuing.
\ The time as number before, e.g. 1000 MS defines the delay time in milliseconds.
: ONOFF PWH 1000 MS PWL ;

: Hello   ." HELLO FORTH WORLD " ;   \ just in addition added, the usual first program people write

The Forth Words used here and a short explanation:
\ SPACE   Print a SPACE to the screen
\ \   The divider – anything after the \ is ignored by the computer up to the end of the line
\ .   Print a value to the screen
\ ." xx " Print the ASCII string string xx to the screen, ended by "
\   and do not forget the space after the first quote
\ :   Start a new word definition; e.g. : Hello ." Hello " ;
\ ;   And finish the new word definition shown above with ;
\ CR   Send a return to the display – one line down, cursor to the left
\ PAGE   Delete all of the information on screen to have a clean screen, the cursor is at the top left
\ VARIABLE Define a new 16 Bit VARIABLE – only the lowest bit is used here in this example
\ !   Store a value into a VARIABLE: XX PW !
\ @   Read the value back from a VARIABLE and print it: PW @ .
\ MS   MS defines a delay, and the number before MS sets the length: e.g. 100 MS

\ **End of Part 1: success to switch the LED On / Off, and display the result.**
\ **Further parts will be added either online or in the new eBook A Start With Forth part 2.**

5 – Try it out on the web using EASYFORTH

Try out a Forth program without installing anything? No Download either?
There is for example easyFORTH on the internet, a Javascript program which
runs a basic set of Forth words.
To be found at https://skilldrick.github.io/easyforth/
Including a very good description. Just type in the code into the window (
plus <CR>) and run it.
The example from **Imagine to Invent a Language** has to be modified
slightly, but not much.
The list of Forth Words implemented is rather limited, but sufficient to have
a try and get a feeling.
The SNAKE program example included and described in easyFORTH is a
challenge to understand, but a good way to understand how Forth works.

```
: TEXT0 ." INVENT A LANGUAGE, do a samll application v4  ExMark Oct2016 " CR ;
: TEXT1 ." PW " CR ;
: TEXT2 ." 0 " CR ;

VARIABLE PW

: PWH   1 PW ! ;  \ set the variable PW to 1 (HIGH)
: PWL   0 PW ! ;  \ set the variable PW to 0 (LOW)

: DISBIT PW @ . SPACE ;

: BITPW   DISBIT ;

: Display   CR TEXT1 DISBIT ;

: ONOFF  PWH 1000 sleep PWL ; \ change, replace ms by sleep

: Hello  ." HELLO FORTH WORLD " ;
\ End of program
```

6 – Extend the 12 Words to 35 Words

Picture of the first Test Group for the 35 Word Forth – the training took 2 hours and was successful. Actually, this workshop lead to the 12 Words piece described before, to have an even easier Starting Point.

Download for print in different versions from

https://wiki.forth-ev.de/doku.php/en:projects:a-start-with-forth:start

\ Write a simple Application just using 35 Forth Words - set IO bits, start a counter -- ExMark - Juergen Pintaske Oct. 2016
\ There is a Word for SOS as well, but dependent on the hardware you can hear the SOS as some sounds (or not) just try. Easyforth has this word not yet implemented.

\ VFXTESTAPP - A Demo running on the PC. Set up a folder c:\VFXTESTAPP . Store this file VFXTESTAPP.f into this folder

\ (INCLUDE c:\VFXTESTAPP\VFXTESTAPP.f) copy the text in brackets into the VFX window, and hit <cr> to run the demo.

\ VFX reads in the file, VFX compiles new words where needed. SOS should be heard, then a simple "GUI" of few lines shows.

\ and the 4 out bits are counted up. <cr> stops this and answers ok. Now set bits, e.g. with PWL or PWL <cr> otr the others.

\ or try NAME, type SOS <cr>, or COUNTER <cr>, <cr> to get back into command mode; or 400 SCOUNTER <cr> with 400 setting speed

\ Or try the very basic debugger with ???? <cr>

\ Desription: The implementation of a virtual MicroBox, which consists of a Micro, PWM LED, 3 Switches, 4 OUT LEDs, 4 IN LEDs

\ Here just some functionality implemented in SW: no chip, no LEDs, no resistors, no PCB, no soldering – an Application on PC only

\ The "GUI", the Graphic User Interface implemented using two very simple words – Page to clear screen, <cr> go to next line.

\ MMT7 shows the funtions represented, and below MMT7 the 1bit PWM, 3bits SWITCHES, 4bits OUT, 4bits IN, 4bits A – 16 bits

\ Further down find MBV2, it prints the 16 Bits underneath this text. All lines are resent whenever the 16 bits are updated.

\ LINE1 to LINE4 define words to explain the names of the single bits and the control words. LINE4 not used. Modify to show.

\ This has been intentionally written just using simple words and constructs, so anybody can use it as startig point.

\ And as with all Forth programs, this application can be easily modified and extended – and all interactively.

\ BINARY/HEX 0000 0 0001 1 0011 2 0011 3 0100 4 0101 5 0110 6 0111 7 1000 8 1001 9 1010 A 1011 B 1100 C 1101 D 1110 E 1111 F

HEX \ from now on all of the numbers understood to be hex. The LINES n print a small GUI, very basic, just uses PAGE and CR

: LINE1 ." \ VFXTESTAPP – bit change ie. PWH / PWL <cr>, try COUNTER, 400 SCOUNTER, SOS , ???? plus <cr> ExMark Oct2016" CR ;

: LINE2 ." \ PWHL T3HL T2HL T1HL O3HL O2HL O1HL O0HL I3HL I2HL I1HL I0HL A3Hl A2HL A1HL A0HL h/l ???? " CR ;

: **LINE3** ." \ PWM   T3____T2____T1   O3____O2____O1____O0   I3____I2____I1____I0 A3____A2____A1____A0 " CR ;

: **LINE4** ." X t t t o o o o i i i i a a a a " CR ; \ display after START?

: **TEST PAGE LINE1 LINE2 LINE3 LINE4 (LINE5) CR ;** \ display lines of our GUI Graphic User Interface, 5 not used

Variable PWM (0 or 1) \ not used for now as combined in Variable PSWI
Variable SWI (Switches SW3 SW2 SW1 0 0 0) \ not used for now as combined in Variable PSWI
Variable PSWI (Combined PWM and Switches X s s s) \ combines the bit for PWM and the 3 bits for the 3 switches
Variable OUTP (OUTP 3 2 1 0)(same as Bit 7 6 5 4) \ the 4 "OUTPUT LEDs" of the MicroBox
Variable IN (IN 3 2 1 0 (3 2 1 0 of the 8 Bits) \ 4 Input bits that can be set e.g. for AND OR XOR INVERT
Variable ANI (Simulated analog input 0 to F) \ either as simulated external ANALOG - or free for anything
Variable HOU (OUT as hexadecimal number 0 to F) \ to be implemented, just showing the 4 OUT bits in hexadecimal
Variable ALL (PWM SWI OUT INP ANI) \ To be done, combining it all into one 16 bit Variable

: **disbit4** DUP $8 AND IF ." 1" ELSE ." 0" THEN ; \ display a bit, here the topmost of the 4. If 1 then display 1, else 0

: **ds** Disbit4 1 LSHIFT ; \ display a bit and shift the 4 bit left by one, so the next is the topmost

: **dssp** ds Space Space space space ; \ combine a bit to a block with 4 Spaces spaces

: **4dssp** dssp dssp dssp disbit4 drop ; \ now combine all 4 bits of the Variable nibble, DROP cleans up the stack

: **DV** 3 spaces PSWI @ 4dssp 4 spaces OUTP @ 4dssp 4 spaces IN @ 4dssp 4 spaces ANI @ 4dssp ; \ combine 4x 4 = 16 bits

: **SPACES** (u --) 0 ?DO SPACE LOOP ; \ define SPACES, often included in the word set already

: **MBV2** PAGE LINE1 LINE2 LINE3 LINE4 DV CR ; \ MBV2 updates the "SCREEN", first the explaining lines, then the 16 Bits

: **COUNTER** Begin outp @ 1+ outp ! 300 ms mbv2 key? until ; \ run counter program, see OUT bits change, type counter <cr>

: **SCOUNTER** Begin dup outp @ 1+ outp !   ms mbv2 key? until ; \ programmable speed, for example 400 scounter <cr>

: **SOS** 07 emit 100 ms 07 emit 100 ms 07 emit 600 ms 07 emit 300 ms 07 emit 300 ms 07 emit 600 ms 07 emit 100 ms 07 emit 100 ms 07 emit ; / 07 is the Bel command

: **LINE5** ." PSWI OUT IN   ANI - R0 R1   - Stack contents   " CR ; \ description of ??? display

: **????** 3 spaces PSWI @ . OUTP @ . IN @ . ANI @ . 4 spaces >R >R >R >R >R >R >R >R R> DUP . R> DUP . R> DUP . R> DUP . R> DUP . R> DUP . R> DUP . R> DUP . ; \ ???? displays PSWI OUTP IN ANI and Dstack: 8 levels. Enter FFFF, sets lowest one visible as bottom, so 7 left

: **???** PSWI @ . OUTP @ . IN @ . ANI @ . base @ >r hex .S r> base ! ; \ Debug 2 – prints 4 variables + Data + Stack differently

\ Preset Variables:
0 PWM ! \   not used for now
0 SWI ! \   not used for now
9 PSWI ! \ Set this combined variable to 9 = 1001 this will show the PWM LED ON and SW1 ON
0 OUTP ! \ All bits LOW 0000
3 IN ! \ The IN variable set to 3 0011 - prepared to try AND OR XOR INVERT
F ANI ! \ Set to F but not used for now
F HOU ! \   not used for now
FFFF ALL ! \   ALL will be the combined 16 Bit Vector PWSI OUT IN ANI later , was commented out here for now

\ Control Words (from left to right as shown in MMT3 and MMT4)

: PWH PSWI @ $8 OR PSWI ! MBV2 ; \ Get the variable onto stack, set bit 3, and store it back, now update the Display
: T3H PSWI @ $4 OR   PSWI ! MBV2 ; \ Get the variable onto stack, set bit 2, and store it back, see above
: T2H PSWI @ $2 OR PSWI ! MBV2 ; \ And the same for setting all of the other bits
: T1H PSWI @ $1 OR PSWI ! MBV2 ;
: O3H OUTP @ $8 OR OUTP ! MBV2 ; \ x x x x   1 0 0 0
: O2H OUTP @ $4 OR OUTP ! MBV2 ; \   0 1 0 0
: O1H OUTP @ $2 OR OUTP ! MBV2 ; \   0 0 1 0
: O0H OUTP @ $1 OR OUTP ! MBV2 ; \   0 0 0 1
: I3H IN @ $8 OR IN ! MBV2 ;
: I2H IN @ $4 OR IN ! MBV2 ;
: I1H IN @ $2 OR IN ! MBV2 ;
: I0H IN @ $1 OR IN ! MBV2 ;

```
: A3H  ANI  @  $8 OR  ANI  !  MBV2 ;
: A2H  ANI  @  $4 OR  ANI  !  MBV2 ;
: A1H  ANI  @  $2 OR  ANI  !  MBV2 ;
: A0H  ANI  @  $1 OR  ANI  !  MBV2 ;  \ here end the words that Set Bits HIGH – the next ones set
the same bits LOW

: PWL  PSWI @  $7 AND  PSWI !  MBV2 ; \ xxxx 0 1 1 1
: T3L  PSWI @  $B AND  PSWI !  MBV2 ; \     1 0 1 1
: T2L  PSWI @  $D AND  PSWI !  MBV2 ; \     1 1 0 1
: T1L  PSWI @  $E AND  PSWI !  MBV2 ; \     1 1 1 0
: O3L  OUTP @  $7 AND  OUTP !  MBV2 ;
: O2L  OUTP @  $B AND  OUTP !  MBV2 ;
: O1L  OUTP @  $D AND  OUTP !  MBV2 ;
: O0L  OUTP @  $E AND  OUTP !  MBV2 ;
: I3L  IN  @  $7 AND  IN  !  MBV2 ;
: I2L  IN  @  $B AND  IN  !  MBV2 ;
: I1L  IN  @  $D AND  IN  !  MBV2 ;
: I0L  IN  @  $E AND  IN  !  MBV2 ;
: A3L  ANI  @  $7 AND  ANI  !  MBV2 ;
: A2L  ANI  @  $B AND  ANI  !  MBV2 ;
: A1L  ANI  @  $D AND  ANI  !  MBV2 ;
: A0L  ANI  @  $E AND  ANI  !  MBV2 ;
```

\ Set I1 and/or I0 of the INPUTs, then call AND01, OR01, XOR01, INVERT0, see the result of the logic result in O0

```
: AND01   IN @  DUP 1 RSHIFT AND  01 AND  OUTP !  MBV2 ;  \ Do an AND of IN bit0 and bit1,
00=>1 01=>0 10=>0 11=>1
: OR01   IN @  DUP 1 RSHIFT OR  01 AND  OUTP !  MBV2 ;  \ Do an OR  of IN bit0 and bit1, 00=>0
01=>1 10=>1 11=>1
: XOR01   IN @  DUP 1 RSHIFT XOR  01 AND  OUTP !  MBV2 ;  \ Do an XOR of IN bit0 and bit1,
00=>0 01=>1 10=>1 11=>0
: INVERT0  IN @  INVERT      01 AND  OUTP !  MBV2 ;  \ Do an INV of IN bit0,      0=>1 1=>0
```

\ **List of the 35 Forth Words used – remember:**
\ **Any Forth Word consists of a character sequence plus a space to separate it from the next word**
\ **(not allowed within Words are CR, BS, Space)**

\ **0 INCLUDE**   INCLUDE loads and starts a file in VFX; set up c:\VFXTESTAPP, store file there,stype INCLUDE c:\VFXTESTAPP\VFXTESTAPP.f

\ **1 HEX**   Mostly VFX recognizes numbers as decimal or HEX. If in DECIMAL mode any Hex Number will give an error. Careful!

\ **2 **   \ and a Space after it tells Forth, that the rest of the line is for documentation, so is ignored by VFX.

\ **3 :** : starts new Forth Word definition, is terminated by ; see Number 6. Example : Bell 07 EMIT ; sends a sound.

\ **4 ."** ." and a space starts a string of characters to be sent to the screen, the string is terminated by "

\ **5 CR** CR defines a word that places the cursor to the beginning of the next line

\ **6 ;** ; ends the definition started by : see number 3

\ **7 TEST** TEST is the name of a new word defined just to display the GUI – the Graphical User Interface

\ **8 Variable** Variables = named memory locations. VARIABLE xx defines, nn xx ! sets, xx @ . prints. NAME and contents

\ **9 DUP** DUP takes the value on top of the stack and puts the same value on top as NEW TOS – Top of Stack

\ **10 $n** $n – the $ ensures that VFX takes the number following as hexadecimal number

\ **11 AND** AND is a logical operator. works on the two top numbers on the stack, on a bitwise basis, only leaves result

\ **12 IF** IF not zero do A ELSE do B THEN continue

\ **13 ELSE**

\ **14 THEN**

\ **15 LSHIFT** LSHIFT does a bitwise shift of the value on stack, expects the number of shifts to be done on stack – 1 LSHIFT

\ **16 SPACE** SPACE sends a space to the screen

\ **17 DROP** DROP does the opposite to DUP; DROP takes the TOS and deletes what was there, all values move up one position

\ **18 DV** DV is a word that will send the combined variables to the screen, 16 Bit wide.

\ **19 @** @ stands for AT, for example with Variables – xx puts the address of xx onto the stack, xx @ replaces with value

\ **20 ?DO** ?DO will start a DO word word LOOP, expects the number of loops on stack. ?DO checks if number on stack is 0.

\ **21 LOOP**   Goes back to ?DO until 0, then continues

\ **22 PAGE**   PAGE clears the screen, takes the cursor to the top left position and prints ok

\ **23 BEGIN**   BEGIN starts a loop of words which ends with UNTIL. UNTIL expects a flag on stack; not 0 to BEGIN or continues

\ **24 1+**   1+ is put on stack, adds one to the number below and replaces it. Same function as 1 + as 2 words.

\ **25 !**   ! is the opposite function to @, and stores the number on stack at a location on stack, e.g. 55 xx ! at Variable

\ **26 MS**   MS stands 1 Millisecond delay in software. Careful which base you are in - 256 and 100 the same Dec / HEX

\ **27 KEY?**   Key? Checks, if a key has been pushed as this generates a flag. BEGIN xxxxxxxx KEY? UNTIL - flag stops the loop

\ **28 UNTIL**   UNTIL end the BEGIN ... UNTIL loop, exit if flag true.

\ **29 EMIT**   (07 for Bell) to get audible output from the PC - (:) BELL 07 BEL (;)sends the bell signal to the speaker

\ **30 .S**   .S is a non-destructive display of the stack, and all of the items

\ **31 .**   . is similar, prints out the top item only and as well consumes it; an easy way to get rid of the top stack item

\ **32 >R**   >R takes an item from DSTACK and moves to the RSTACK;

\ **33 R>**   R> does the opposite: take item from RSTACK move it to the DSTACK

\ **34 (and)**   These 2 brackets are used to put explanations within the code, and this is ignored by Forth, imilar to \

\ **35 " is needed together with number 4 ." and ends the string to be sent**

\ ------ it seems this covers all of the words needed in this little application
\

\ **This application has not been programmed optimally - but this was not the target - beginner's code for beginners**
\ Links to further information there : see WORD file and PDF version of this application

```
\
: Name  ." Hello Forth World " ;
Page CR Name   1000 ms
sos    \ send  SOS     and then start the counter
counter \ start COUNTER
```

\ The Forth Machine: Data stream coming in, THE STACK, Return Stack, Variables in memory, other memory, route to output.

\

\ The Forth Machine looks very complicated − but people actually use a similar model every day at their desk, work coming in from the left as tokens, execute directly or, 2 stacks on desk, one for general work, save if interrupted on the second one, use pidgeon holes (Variables), memory - scribbled on paper, results out.

\	DATA_IN	TOP_OF_D_STACK		TOP_OF_RS	x7	DATA_OUT	
\		DS-1		RS-1	x6		
\		DS-2		RS-2	x5		
\		DS-3		RS-3	x4		
\		DS-4		RS-4	PSWI	x3	
\		DS-5		RS-5	OUTP	x2	
\		DS-6		RS-6	IN	x1	
\	Token8 7 6 5 4 3 2 1 0	FFFF	(-7)	FFFF	ANI	x0	OUT
\							
\	Input_Buffer_Contents	DATA_S	RETURN_S	VARIABLES	MEM	OUT	

7 – Now use downloadable VFXTESTAPP.exe

Having used the web based easyFORTH as a first start, let us now do the next step and run Forth code interactively.

Normally you would have to install a Forth compiler like VFX. MPE has been very kind and generated a VFXTESTAPP.exe for download, which has similar functionality.

You can download VFXTESTAPP.exe from our dropbox at vfxtestapp.exe or via https://wiki.forth-ev.de/doku.php/en:projects:a-start-with-forth:start

where you can find more documentation. Just generate a folder on your PC if you want to keep it.

To have your work available next time use SAVE onto your PC.

To have full access to the MPE VFX Forth compiler, download and install from the MPE website

http://www.mpeforth.com/arena.htm

Then you have as well access to the full documentation as PDF.

The same manual can also be downloaded from the starting point

35 Forth Words as First Entry Application at https://wiki.forth-ev.de/doku.php/en:projects:a-start-with-forth:start

8 – MPE Forth Tool AIDE with ForthED2
As Part of the VFX MSP430 LITE

After Installation – try the 12 Word Forth as test using the DFX console, see screen prints

```
DFX Debug console                                              _ □ X

MPE VFX Forth
DFX console started

  ok
  ok
  ok
: Hello   ." Hello Forth World " ;   ok
hello Hello Forth World   ok
  ok
: TEXT0 ." INVENT A LANGUAGE, do a samll application ExMark 2016_11_27   " (
: TEXT1 ." PW " CR ;   ok
: TEXT1 ." PW " CR ;
TEXT1 is redefined   ok
VARIABLE PW    ok
: PWH 1 PW ! ;   ok
: PWL 0 PW ! ;   ok
: BITPW   PW @ .  ;        ok
: Display  CR TEXT1 BITPW ;   ok
: PULSELED  PWH Display  1000 MS PWL display ;   ok
: Hello ." HELLO FORTH WORLD " ;
HELLO is redefined   ok
  ok
  ok
text0 INVENT A LANGUAGE, do a samll application ExMark 2016_11_27
  ok
text1 PW
  ok
display
PW
0  ok
1 PW !   ok
display
PW
1  ok
0 PW !   ok
display
PW
0  ok
pulseled
PW
1
PW
0  ok
  ok
  ok
hello HELLO FORTH WORLD   ok
```

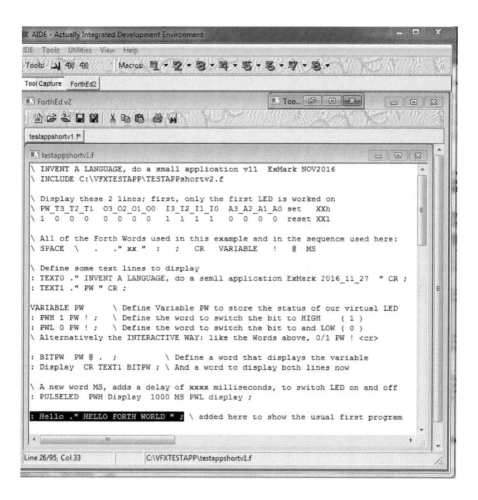

And then the the the 35 Words application – or your own Forth code

MPE Forth

AIDE

Actually Integrated
Development Environment

User Manual

AIDE

User manual

Manual revision 6.8
Date 02 September 2016
a5v1

Software

Software version 6.8

Package Number:	

For technical support

Please contact your supplier

For further information

MicroProcessor Engineering Limited
133 Hill Lane, Southampton, SO15 5AF, UK
Tel: +44 (0)23 8063 1441
Fax: +44 (0)23 8033 9691
e-mail: mpe@mpeforth.com tech-support@mpeforth.com
web: www.mpeforth.com

Table of Contents

What is AIDE?

Pronounced "AIDE"

AIDE is a modular integrated development environment for the MPE series of tools and compiler. It provides a framework from which to use two types of tools.

1. MPE supplied compiler tools
2. External User tools

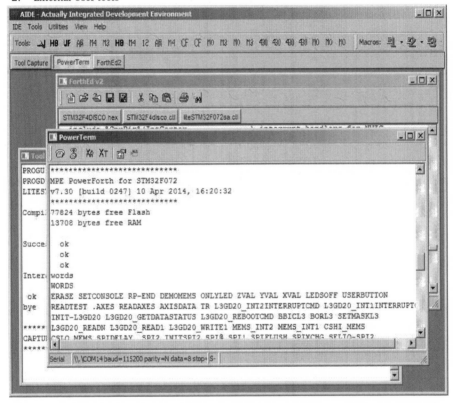

AIDE is written in Forth and the source code is available on request.

The Main IDE Frame

The main IDE consists of a single window frame with a "Tool Capture Display" Window (*See Capturing External Tools*).

The IDE provides the necessary functionality to:

- Launch both MPE and User supplied tools (*See External Tools*)
- Configure text substitution macros for use in command lines to launch tools.
- Automatically include and maintain "plugin" tools.

The Main Menu Bar

The *IDE* Menu

This menu provides options for general configuration of the IDE. Available sub-options are:

Configure

Setup general IDE options, especially the editor and **LOCATE** facilities. Within the editor configuration string 'f' will be replaced by the file name and 'l' will be replaced by the line number, for example:

```
CodeWright     "%f%" -g%l%
Crimson        /L:%l% "%f%"
Ed4Windows     -1 -n -1 %l% "%f%"
               N.B. the first is minus 1

EMACS          --no-wait +%l% "%f%"
PFE32          /G%L% "%f%"
Programmer's Notepad
               -1 %l% "%f%"
UltraEdit      "%f%" -l%l%
WinEdit        "%f%" -# %l%
```

Editor path names containing spaces must be entered surrounded by quotes in the IDE->Configure dialog box. We have worked around some problems with the Windows API when saving these path names. When entering the locate command string in this dialog you must put quotes around the **%f%** macro in order to handle filenames containg spaces. If you do this, you must also specify the line macro **%l%** to prevent Windows from removing the quote marks. The following (for UltraEdit) works:

"%f%" -l%l%

but

"%f%"

will eventually fail.

To help you configure **LOCATE**, there's a checkbox to produce debug information. The display format is crude, so please remember to to uncheck this when **LOCATE** is working properly.

Macro Management	Alter the names and alternatives for the built in text macros.
External Tools	Configure and manage external tool options.
Save INI file as ...	The working INI file is saved .
	You have to enter a file name for the saved file.
Load INI file from ...	Enter a file name, and when AIDE is next restarted, the given file is copied to the working INI file.
Exit	Closes AIDE.

The *Tools* Menu

This menu contains a list of the currently configured external tools. Selecting an item here will run the specified tool. This menu is also reflected as a toolbar within the IDE.

The *Utilities* Menu

This menu contains internal tools. Selecting an item here will run the specified tool.

The default options are:

Calculator
Run the usual Windows calculator.

ASCII Chart
Display the ASCII table in hex, decimal, and control code descriptions.

BMP to LCD Converter
Convert picture in .BMP format to a native LCD format.

Tool Capture
If ticked, the tool capture window is open.

PowerTerm
If ticked, the PowerTerm window is open. You can toggle this.

ForthEd2
If ticked, the ForthEd2 window is open. You can toggle this.

Forth Console
If clicked, a Forth console opens.

Go Online
Launch your web browser.

The *Help* Menu

This menu provides various information and help options such as MPE contact details, product version information and manuals.

The Main Window "CoolBar"

In addition to the main window menu the IDE frame also provides three toolbars organized in a "coolbar" format. Two of these toolbars echo the functionality and options of the ***Tools*** and the ***Help*** sub-menus. The third toolbar provides control for the text substitution macros. (*See Text Substitution Macros*)

Configuring and Maintaining Forth

About External Tools

An *External Tool* is simply another program outside AIDE which is invoked in a specified manner from within AIDE by clicking a button on the toolbar or from the **Tools** menu. These tools can be DOS tools, Console Mode apps or Windows GUI applications. Simple "fire-and-forget" tools such as MAKE can have their input and output revectored to an IDE window rather than a separate console. There is a limit of 26 tools which can be added to the IDE. The tool management dialog is invoked by the "**External Tools**" option on the **IDE** menu.

You **must** use the *Save* button before the *Exit* button when you change an item in the dialog.

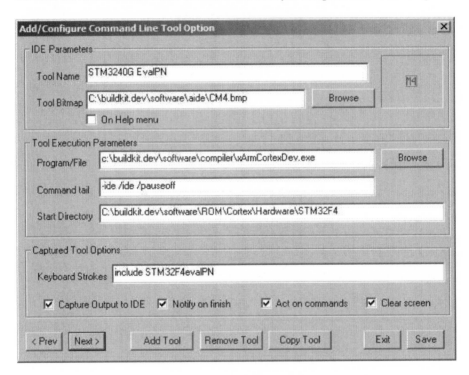

IDE Parameters

These are the options which control how the tool is represented within the main IDE Frame.

Tool Name

The name is the tool name as it will appear on the *TOOL* menu and tooltips.

Tool Bitmap

A path to the image file to use on the coolbar to represent the tool. A ***Browse*** button is supplied for locating bitmap images. The bitmap must be 16 color (Windows) and must be 16*16 pixels in size. If you want to create buttons yourself, you can do this with the Paint program, *mspaint.exe*.

Help Item checkbox

If this box is checked, the tool will appear on the Help menu. Note that any program can be launched this way, and so this is a useful way of accessing project information such as chip data sheets which are normally provided as PDF files. See " ***Command Line***" below for more details.

Tool Execution Parameters

These parameters control how the tool is to be launched.

Program/File

This box contains the command line for executing the tool. This can be either a full path or a path relative to the *Start Directory* as defined below.

Command Tail

Command Line options can be added and text macros can be used to form part or all of the command line.

If your tool has a space in the path, e.g. it is somewhere in the *Program Files* folder, you should separate the program name and keep it here. Put the rest of the command line in the "*Command tail*" box.

If you just want to display a web page or a PDF file, and you have an association set up (you do by default), just put the full pathname here, leave "*Command tail*" box empty and put a single dot in the "*Start Directory*" box

Start Directory

This represents a full path which will form the current working directory when the tool is launched.

Captured Tool Options

These parameters control input/output redirection of command line tools to the IDE.

Keyboard Strokes

Only valid for a captured tool. Any text in this box is passed to STDIN of the tool after it is launched.

Capture Output To IDE

When checked, all console IO for this tool will be redirected to the IDE capture window.

Notify on finish

When checked, a banner is displayed in the capture window when the tool terminates.

Act on Commands

Enables AIDE to react to AIDE-specific commands from the tool. The MPE Forth Cross Compilers use this feature to launch the editor and to display the source for Forth words.

Clear screen

The IDE capture window will be cleared before the tool is run.

Other Buttons

Prev

Cycle display to the previous external tool.

Next

Cycle display to the next defined external tool.

Add Tool

Add a new blank tool entry. The options can then be filled in.

Remove Tool

Delete the current tool entry. Note that the last tool in the list (Explorer) cannot be removed.

Copy Tool

Create a new tool entry and fill its configuration with that of the previous current tool.

Exit

Leave this dialog.

Save

Apply changes to current tool. NOTE: Changes are not committed any other way. If you fail to *Save* changes before using Add, Next etc. **they will be forgotten**.

Upgrading from previous version of AIDE

If you are upgrading from a previous version of AIDE which did not have the *"Command Tail"* entry, you will have to update your configurations manually. Don't forget to press *"Save"* for each one.

Where you previously had a *"Command Line"* entry:

    c:\buildkit.dev\software\compiler\xmsp430.exe /ide /pauseoff

split this into the two entries *"Program/File"* and *"Command tail"*

    c:\buildkit.dev\software\compiler\xmsp430.exe /ide /pauseoff

If you are also upgrading to a version 7 Forth cross compiler, the Command Tail entry should be changed to:

    -ide /ide /pauseoff

where the -ide switch causes the VFX Forth host to configure itself for AIDE, and the /ide switch causes the cross compiler to use AIDE to launch the editor for **LOCATE** commands.

Merging INI files

AIDE saves its configuration in a file called *Aide.ini*. This file is kept in a directory called *%AppData%\MPE\Aide*, where *%AppData%* is operating system and user specific, for example for one MPE box, *%AppData%* expands to *C:\Users\Stephen\AppData\Local*. A side effect of this is that Aide.ini is global to all instances of AIDE. See below for using separate configuration files.

This can cause trouble when you install a new cross-compiler. Because there is already a file called *%AppData%\MPE\Aide*, a new one is not copied from the directory containing AIDE. However, it is not difficult to extract the external tool information from the new *Aide.ini* and add it to the existing one. There are two approaches to performing the merge. One is to print out the new INI file and manually enter the data using the IDE->External Tools Dialog. The other is to edit the old INI file directly.

Editing *Aide.ini*

Shutdown all copies of AIDE.

Find the new *aide.exe* and you will find another *Aide.ini* in the same directory.

In the new *Aide.ini*, copy the text describing the external compilers. These are of the form:

```
eaaadwtype            = 2
eaaasztoolname        = STM32-P107
eaaaszbitmapcolor     =
C:\buildkit.dev\software\aide\CM3.bmp
eaaaidcommand         = 58720
eaaaszcommandline     =
c:\buildkit.dev\software\compiler\xArmCortexDev.exe eaaaszcommandtail    = -ide /ide /pauseoff
eaaaszstartdirectory  =
C:\buildkit.dev\software\ROM\Cortex\Hardware\STM32
eaaaszkeystroke       = include STM32-P107.ctl
```

eaaabcaptured	= -1
eaaadwactionontermination	= -1
eaaapreclear	= -1
eaaabhelpitem	= 0
eaaabactcommand	= -1

Each line corresponds to an entry in the IDE->External Tools dialog.

Each tool description line starts with Xaaa, where X runs from A..Z and must be contiguous. Now place all the tools you want in *%AppData%\MPE\Aide\Aide.ini*, Edit the first letter of each tool line so that each tool has a unique character and these characters are contiguous.

Save the file and restart AIDE.

Using separate configuration files

When you have several copies of AIDE and want each one to use its own INI file, launch the secondary copies of AIDE with the *-ini-exec* command line switch, e.g.
C:\buildkit.dev\software\aide.dev\aide.exe –ini-exec
and AIDE will run with the INI file in the directory containing *aide.exe*, in this case
 C:\buildkit.dev\software\aide.dev
The switch *-ini-exec* must be in lower case.

This arrangement is particularly useful when you are evaluating compilers such as the Lite versions and do not want to have to merge INI files.

The Tool Capture Display Window

This window is a part of the IDE framework by default. It provides a console, which can act as the IO device for a captured external tool. (See previous section). This window handles the Windows standard cut/copy and paste keyboard shortcuts. It has a right-click context menu.

Pressing the right hand mouse button within the capture window will pop-up a menu giving Cut/Copy/Paste options as well as Print and Text Search facilities.

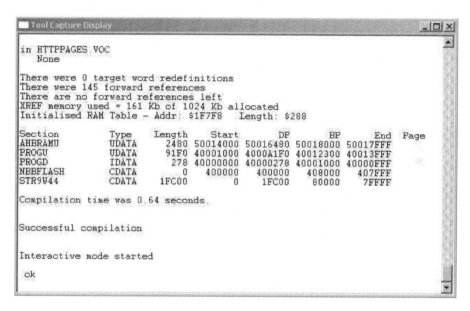

Text Macro Substitutions

About Text Macros

All strings used in the configuration of the IDE and the External tools can have text macro expansion. The IDE provides eight user definable text macros, each of which can have up to eight different translations depending on user selection.

Text macros are used by placing their names (surrounded by percentage character %) within a text string. For example, a text-macro called FRED could form the path to a command line using:

You can define two different versions of this macro, one for use on your desktop, and another for use on your laptop. The availability of these macros allows you to copy folders from desktop to laptop without having to edit source code files.

Note that the MPE Forth cross compilers also support text macros, but the macros within the cross compiler are separate from those used by AIDE. All AIDE macros are expanded (substituted) before the string to passed to the compiler or other external tool.

Changing Macro Names

The IDE provides 8 text macros. The names for these macros can be edited using the dialog provided by the menu option *Macro Management* on the *IDE* sub-menu.

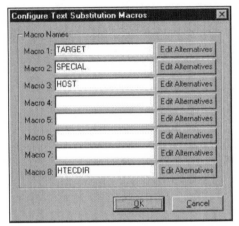

This dialog allows you to change the name of each text macro.

Editing Macro Alternatives

The **Edit Alternatives** buttons allow you to configure the 8 possible alternatives to the translation of each macro.

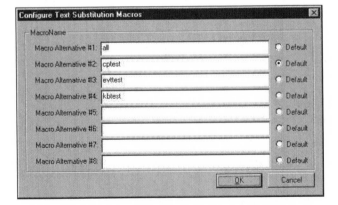

Selecting Active Macro Translation

Since each of the 8 text macros can have up to 8 possible alternative translations the IDE needs to provide a method of switching translations. This can be achieved by entering the **Configure Text Substitution Macros** dialog as before but can also be done via the main IDE "coolbar".

On the main coolbar each macro has a button which can drop-down a menu. The dropdown menu lists the possible alternatives and places a tick next to the currently selected translation. Simply click on the required translation to change.

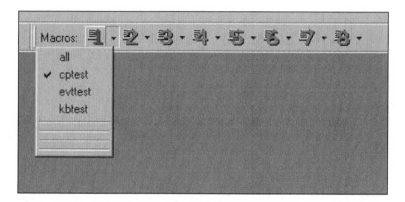

PowerTerm

About PowerTerm

PowerTerm is an RS232 Terminal window for AIDE.

The PowerTerm window has 3 major parts.

1. The toolbar. This provides the Connect/Disconnect, Configure and Logging options

2. The Main Terminal display Window

3. The Status display.

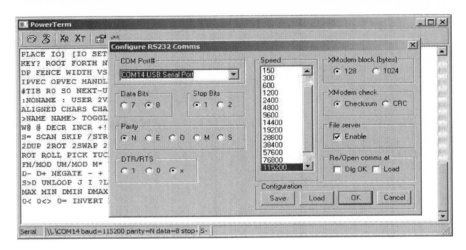

You can get to most of the functions of PowerTerm from a right-click menu.

Toolbar Buttons

Connect

This option will attempt to open the configured serial port.

Disconnect

Close any currently open serial port.

 ### Xmodem Receive/Transmit

These two buttons allow you to receive and transmit binary file in Xmodem format. Xmodem configuration defaults to 128 bytes and checksum. You can change this in the Server and XMODEM panel of the configuration dialog. Transfers using 1024 byte blocks with CRCs are much faster, especially with USB serial ports.

Configure

Change the current configuration of the serial port, Xmodem and the console window. Many USB serial devices need high COM port numbers. You can find out which is which using *Control Panel - > System -> Hardware -> Device Manager -> Ports* or a similar incantation. Recent versions of PowerTerm show the "friendly" device names to make life easier for you

Console window configuration includes enabling and disabling of the file server facilities, which can be used by target hardware using the MPE ROM PowerForth code (usually in the COMMON\ROMFORTH directory). These facilities are documented in the ROM PowerForth manual.

 Log console to file

This is a toggle that controls logging of the console to a file. When logging is enabled, you will be presented with a file selector dialog to select the file for logging. This toggle can also be activated by pressing ^T.

The Status Bar

The first panel indicates the connection status - "Serial" or "Closed".

The second panel shows the connection conditions, e.g. " COM6: baud=115200 parity=N data=8 stop=1".

The third panel contains 'S' if the file server is enabled and 'L' if data is looged to a file.

The fourth panel contains a line number during a file include or a block number during an Xmodem transfer.

Shortcut keys

The following shortcut keys are available:

^C – Copy highlighted text to the clipboard

^V – Paste text from the C[ipboard (also Shift-Insert).

^K – send time and date to the target as a Forth string. This is useful to set the real
time clock of a target board. The format of the string is:
%d to dow %d %d %d %d %d %d SetTime&Date
where %d corresponds to a literal number, **dow** is a Forth **VALUE** containing
the day of the week and the parameters to **SetTime&Date** are as for
Time&Date.

^L – clear the display.

^T – start/stop logging.

^Y – start XModem receiver.

^Z – start XModem-128 transmitter

^\ - start XModem-1024 transmitter

Auxiliary debug displays

The main PowerTerm console is not cursor-addressable, it was designed for logging data. For those occasions when you need an old-fashioned display, or when you need multiple displays for a multitasked application, you can use the auxiliary debug displays. These are traditional cursor-addressable displays.

The displays are controlled by sending control sequences starting with <ESC><!>. Unless otherwise stated parameters are single bytes in the range 0..255. The whole of the command sequence must be performed with inter-character gaps less than 100 ms. For examples of using these commands see the target files *Common\DebugChan.fth* and *Examples\hanoi.fth*.

<ESC>!'0'	Use the main PowerTerm console – char code 0
<ESC>!'1'	Use the the first debug display – char code 1
<ESC>!'2'	Use the the second debug display – char code 2
<ESC>!...	
<ESC>!'8'	Use the the eighth debug display – char code 8
	If a display is not open, it is created.
	If it has not been defined, the default is
	80x25 in a 10 point font.
<ESC>!'9'n	Close display n (1..8).
<ESC>!'10'nwhf	Define the display size and open it
	n is the display in the range 1..8
	w (width) and h (height) are 1..255.
	f (font height) is 6..24
	The display is not selected for output.
<ESC>!'11'n#<txt>	Set the caption of an open display
	n is the display, 1..8
	# is the number of characters in the string
	txt is the string (no terminator)
<ESC>!'12'nfffbbb	Set the foreground and background colours
	n is the display in the range 1..8
	fff is a 24 bit foreground colour
	(big-endian)
	bbb is a 24 bit background colour
	(big-endian)
<ESC>!'13'n	Clear the display to the background colour
	n is the display in the range 1..8
<ESC>!'14'nxy	Goto the given position
	n is the display in the range 1..8
	x is the X position from the left
	y is the Y position from the top

To use these facilities, compile the file *Common\DebugChan.fth* into your target to provide a set of words for accessing the displays. An example using the old Towers of Hanoi as a demonstration can be found in *Examples\hanoi.fth*.

Gotchas

The target should be set up to send the CR character (ASCII code 13) before the LF character (ASCII code 10) for correct display. Unfortunately Windows does not recognise LF before CR as a valid sequence, leading to the display of a curious character instead.

When the file server is enabled, some control characters will trigger the internal file server. If you are debugging a target system that is prone to crash or produce erratic characters, you should disable the file server.

Note that when using USB serial adaptors, especially on laptops, you may need to use *Control Panel* -> *System* -> *Device Manager* to find out which COM port number is to be used. However, PowerTerm's configuration dialog does a good job of listing the 'friendly' names of the COM ports.

Some USB serial adapters, especially generic ones, have simply dreadful Windows device drivers.

Always install the latest drivers for your specific device. We generally buy FTDI cables directly from FTDI. We have also had good results with Keyspan devices. If things go wrong with adapters based on the Prolific chip sets you can always try downloading the latest drivers from Prolific. Assuming that the latest Windows drivers are up to date is a mistake. Yes, we are tired of performing technical support for serial issues caused by bad device drivers.

ForthEd2

About ForthEd2

ForthEd2 is a simple ASCII text editor for AIDE. It allows the simultaneous editing of up to 16 files with full text search, clipboard access and printer support.

ForthEd2 is also linked to remote commands from the tool capture window. If you have enabled the "Act on command channel" checkbox in the external tool configuration, the MPE cross compiler **LOCATE** command will show the source code of the word in ForthEd.

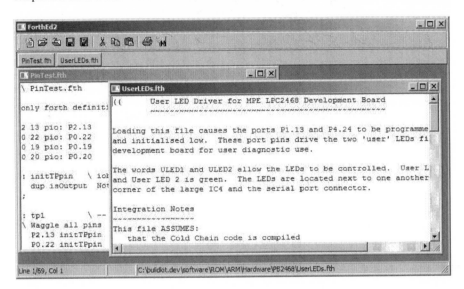

You can get to most of the functions of ForthEd2 from a right-click menu.

Note that ForthEd2 is **not** a production-grade programmer's editor. It's provided because IDEs have to have an editor, so AIDE has one! There are plenty of really good programmers editors available at very low cost. MPE's current favourite is *UltradEdit* from *www.ultraedit.com*.

Display/Edit Window

The editors main display window consists of a tabbed control area. Each file currently open has a tab, which you can use to navigate from file to file.

Toolbar Buttons

New File
Create a new blank file and select it.

Open File
Create a new tab window and load in the contents of a given text file.

Close File
Close the currently active text file. This option does **not** perform a *Save*.

Save File
Save the current text file. The name to be used for the destination file is the same as the tab control title. The file is **not** closed.

Save File As
Save the current text file. The editor will ask for a filename.

Cut
Cut the selected text into the Windows clipboard.

Copy
Copy the selected text to the Windows clipboard.

Paste
Paste text from the Windows clipboard to the current cursor position.

Print
Print the current file.

Search
Search the currrent file for text strings.

Shortcut keys

The following shortcut keys are available while editing:

^S – save
^C – copy to clipboard
^X – copy to clipboard and delete
^V – paste from clipboard (also Shift–Insert)
^F – Find/Search
^N – New
^O – Open
^P – Print

MPE Forth Cross-Compiler and AIDE

The MPE Cross-Compilers have built-in support for the AIDE development environment.

Command line switches

By default, an MPE cross-compiler is a standalone Windows GUI program. There are switches which can be appended to the cross-compiler command line in order to run it as a captured external tool from within AIDE.

Forth 7

The relevant switches are:

-IDE　　　　　Run compiler as a Win32 Console Application. Must be the first item on the command tail

/PAUSEOFF　　Close down compiler when compilation complete.

/IDE　　　　　Use AIDE for **LOCATE**.

Forth 6

The relevant switches are:

/IDE　　　　　Run compiler as a Win32 Console Application. Must be the first entry on the command tail)

/PAUSEOFF　　Close down compiler when compilation complete.

ForthEd2

ForthEd2 can be linked to remote commands from the compiler. If you have enabled the *"Act on command channel"* checkbox in the external tool configuration, the cross compiler **LOCATE** command will show the source code of the word in ForthEd2. Setting the **INTERACTIVE** and **+XREFS** switches in your control file, and then using the **XREF <name>** and **LOCATE <name>** facilities provides very powerful and quick source management facilities.

Umbilical Forth Serial Comms

When using the Umbilical Forth system you should not use *PowerTerm* to access the target board. If the terminal is active the live-Forth in the cross-compiler cannot use that serial port to make the umbilical link. **Disconnect PowerTerm before using Umbilical Forth.**

Stand-alone Forths

PowerTerm can be used with all MPE stand-alone Forths.

ROM PowerForth

PowerTerm includes facilities that allow targets built by the MPE Forth6 and VFX cross compilers to compile source code directly from the host PC. These are described fully in the ROM PowerForth manual. Note that the Forth6 target ROMFORTH code is **not** compatible with the code for the earlier XShell front ends.

UP-LOAD   (--)

PowerTerm will ask you which file you wish to send, and the file will then be compiled. Note that because this protocol also works with other terminal emulators, the last line in the file **must** include the word **END-UP-LOAD**.

GET <filename>   ("<filename>" --)
INCLUDE <filename>   ("<filename>" --)

Running these on the target triggers the file server to download source code which is compiled by the target. Files may be nested and require no special terminating condition.

HEX-DOWN   (addr len --)

Transmits an intel hex file to the host. PowerTerm can capture this using the logging function.

BIN-DOWN   (addr len --)

Triggers the XMODEM receiver in PowerTerm. The name of the file to be created will asked for by PowerTerm.

Custom versions of AIDE

AIDE is written in Forth, specifically for VFX Forth for Windows.

If you want to customise AIDE yourself, you can get the source code for AIDE by obtaining a Developer edition of a cross compiler. Then ask MPE for the source code if it was not provided with the cross compiler. You may have to sign a Non-Disclosure Agreement (NDA).

Index

9 – VFX 430 LITE – Run Forth on a TI MSP430

MSP430 Lite Target Code

v7.3

Microprocessor Engineering Limited

Copyright ©2003, 2005, 2007, 2009, 2013
Microprocessor Engineering Limited
MSP430 Lite Target Code v7.3 Manual revision 7.3
10 November 2014
133 Hill Lane – Southampton SO15 5AF UK
Tel: +44 (0)23 8063 1441 – e-mail: mpe@mpeforth.com

Table of Contents

1 Lite Version Licence Terms

1.1 Compiler

You may not redistribute any portion of the compiler or Lite system distribution without written permission from MicroProcessor Engineering Ltd (MPE). The distribution should be downloaded as a whole from the MPE web site.

The compiler is licensed for non-commercial uses only. For example, you may not sell a product that contains code generated with the Lite compiler. If your job or payment depends on use of the Lite compiler, that is a commercial use.

If you think that you are a special case, e.g. you want to use the compiler in a school, college or university class, just ask us.

If you are not a special case, use the Lite compiler for evaluation and then buy a Standard or Professional version of the compiler to acquire many more facilities and a commercial-use licence.

1.2 Distribution of application programs

Applications compiled with the MPE Lite compiler may be distributed free-of-charge. The MPE sign-on message must be preserved and a link to the MPE website must be provided. No part of the cross-compiler or the target source code may be further distributed except as detailed above.

1.3 Warranties and support

We try to make our products as reliable and bug free as we possibly can. We support our products. If you find a bug in this product and its associated programs we will do our best to fix it. Please check first by email to tech-support@mpeforth.com to see if the problem has already been fixed. Please send us enough information including source code on disc or by email to us, so that we can replicate the problem and then fix it. Please let us know the version/build number of your system.

Technical support will only be available on the current version of the product.

2 Introduction

This manual documents the MPE Forth kernel for the MSP430 Launchpad with anMSP430G2553 processor.

2.1 Before you start

The MPE Forth kernel uses the hardware UART for serial communications. This is run through the USB facilities on the Launchpad. Make sure that the five links of J3 and the two links of J5 on the Launchpad are set as below.

Figure 2.1: Launchpad links

Check that the TI DLLs, *MSP430.dll* and *HIL.dll* are installed where the MPE cross-compiler can find them. Installation is dicussed in chapter 4, "JTAG and and the MSP430" of the MSP40 cross-compiler manual, *Docs/MSP430man.pdf*. If the DLLs are incorrectly installed, you will not be able to program the Launchpad with the Forth kernel.

2.2 Working with AIDE

It seems to be essential that every language has an IDE. If you do not like IDEs, you can skip this section. AIDE has three parts:

• Editor - ForthEd2 is a trivial editor just so that AIDE has one. There are many far better programming editors. You can get AIDE to use a different one using the *IDE -> Configure/Locate* menu entry. See the AIDE manual for more details.

• Tool Capture Display - the cross compiler window in most cases. Note that this is software running on the host PC. For a standalone Forth target there is no connection to the target, except for Flash programming and all target commands must be entered in a terminal emulator, usually AIDE's PowerTerm. For an Umbilical Forth target, you can enter target commands and the cross compiler will try to execute them on the target.

• PowerTerm - a terminal emulator used with standalone Forth systems. It is specially adapted for debugging complex targets and features up to eight individually controllable cursor-addressable displays - ideal for debugging multi-tasking targets.

2.3 Producing the kernel

The Forth kernel is built using a cross compiler running in the AIDE environment. AIDE contains three primary windows: compiler, terminal emulator and text editor. The compilation results can be seen in the compiler window. During compilation, the compilation results can be seen in the compiler/tool window.

To compile the standalone Forth kernel, find the "liteLP2553sa" button in the main toolbar and click it to compile from the control file *liteLP2553sa.ctl*. The compiler will ask you whether you want to program the Launchpad with the new kernel. Answer 'Y' to the download and erase prompts.

After programming the Launchpad, the new kernel will be running. To talk to the kernel, use AIDE's PowerTerm terminal emulator. The kernel talks to PowerTerm through the Launchpad's application UART. Finding this UART can require a little botheration. There are two ways to do this.

1. Go to Windows Control Panel -> System -> Device Manager -> Ports. One of the entries will be something like: MSP430 Application UART (COM10). COM10 will be the UART you will use.

2. Go to AIDE's PowerTerm configuration dialog. Select the drop down list in the COMPort# group. It will list all the available COM ports by COM number and name. The one you want includes: COMxx MSP430 Application UART.

Now select the required port in the PowerTerm configuration dialog and ensure that it is set to 9600 baud, 8 data bits, 1 stop bit, no parity and file server enabled. Save the configuration and press OK. Start the PowerTerm connection and you should be talking to the kernel.

2.4 About the standalone kernel

The control file *liteLP2553sa.ctl* specifies the use of the target Flash as follows:

Kernel:	$D000..FFE0, then vectors to $FFFF
App:	$C000..CFFF

The App space is where the target kernel compiles code.

The Forth kernel you have made and installed is a cut-down version of the full MPE Forth kernel. It has extensions so that code is compiled directly into the MSP430 Flash. When you want to add code, you can compile it directly on the Forth kernel by using the phrase include <filename>
on the target Forth command line. AIDE will then try to deliver the file to the kernel. If the file cannot be found, AIDE will let you change the default directory (the commonest problem) or correct the spelling.

To start over just type EMPTY, the application region of the Flash will be cleaned, and the CPU is rebooted. To reuse your compiled code at the next reboot or power up, use the word COMMIT. If you just want to preserve the code, use:
Chapter 2: Introduction

0 COMMIT

If you want the Forth to run a word, say APP, use:

' APP COMMIT

2.5 About Umbilical Forth
The control file *liteLP2553uf.ctl* specifies the use of an Umbilical Forth system in which the cross compiler provides all the interactivity. Because the TI Launchpad uses a very slow USB connection, the interaction takes a very long time. It was designed for use with a 115200 baud serial line.
Umbilical Forth provides a minimal Forth system on the target for situations where every byte matters. You can put far more functionality onto a 16 kb Umbilical Forth system than on a 16 kb standalone Forth.

2.6 Gotchas

2.6.1 Flash problems
If you forget to use COMMIT and EMPTY appropriately, the MSP430 Flash may not be correctly erased and so application compilation may fail. Try to use EMPTY and if that fails, reinstall a new kernel.
The Flash programming DLLs are unreliable on many PCs. Just accept this as the cost of cheap hardware and software. Eventually, the Flash will be programmed, but you may need to recompile a few times to achieve this.

The Launchpad is built down to a price. The JTAG facilities are provided by a secondary CPU on the Launchpad and by Windows DLLs. In the past this combination has shown a few problems, especially if the Launchpad has been unexpectedly disconnected and reconnected.

If you come across such a problem, shut down all the software that could be using the MSP430 DLLs. Then restart the software. If problems persist, disconnect the Launchpad, reboot the PC, reconnect the Launchpad, and only then restart the software.

2.6.2 Serial lockup

Occasionally the connection to the USB UART refuses to open properly and AIDE's PowerTerm appears to lock up. DO NOT CLOSE THE CONNECTION. Instead, remove the USB cable and wait for PowerTerm to detect this and close the connection. Then reconnect the USB cable and attempt to open the UART again. You may have to do this a few times to establish a good connection.

3 MSP430G2553 start up

The file *MSP430\Hardware\Launchpad2553\start2553.fth* contains Forth start up code and initialisation tables for a Launchpad board with an MSP430G2553 CPU.

3.1 Magic addresses

Some factory calibration data is held in Info Flash in TLV (Tag, Length, Value) format. The most interesting of this are the DCO and ADC calibration data. For startup, we need the DCO calibration data

$10FF	CALBC1_1MHz
$10FE	CALDCO_1MHz
$10FD	CALBC1_8MHz
$10FC	CALDCO_8MHz
$10FB	CALBC1_12MHz
$10FA	CALDCO_12MHz
$10F9	CALBC1_16MHz
$10F8	CALDCO_16MHz
$10F7 08	Size (bytes) of value data
$10F6 01	Tag

Port 1 is used as follows:

P1.0	Green LED, high=on
P1.1	UART Rx
P1.2	UART Tx
P1.3	Button Switch input
P1.4	– –
P1.5	– –
P1.6	Red LED, high=on
P1.7	– –

3.2 Start of Forth

This section contains initial values of Forth registers and the code to initialise and run Forth.

L: ECLD

The entry point after reset. This code is for a TI Launchpad board run from the DCo at 8 MHz. It uses LEDs on P1.6 (red) and P1.0 (green) for debugging.

XT2-speed [if]

If the equate XT2-speed is set non-zero in the control file, the main clock is taken from the high frequency oscillator at the frequency specified by XT2-speed.

3.3 Default Interrupt vectors

All interrupt vectors are set to point to the ECLD entry point above. Later code may modify these settings.

ECLD reset_vec	**!**
ECLD nmi_vec	**!**
ECLD timer1_A0_vec	**!**
ECLD timer1_A1_vec	**!**
ECLD CompA_vec	**!**
ECLD WDT_vec	**!**
ECLD timer0_a0_vec	**!**
ECLD timer0_a1_vec	**!**
ECLD UCx0Rx_vec	**!**
ECLD UCx0Tx_vec	**!**
ECLD ADC10_vec	**!**
ECLD P2_vec	**!**
ECLD P1_vec	**!**

3.4 Reset values for user and system variables

The equate SP-GUARD in the control file defines how many guard cells are provided at the top of the data stack to give some protection against system crashes if code underflows the data stack. If SP-GUARD is undefined at this point, a default value of 0 is defined.

0 equ sp-guard \ -- n

Default number of data stack guard cells.

The section of USER variable initialisation values is generated for standalone targets if the equate UMBILICAL? is udefined or set to zero.

4 MSP430 code definitions

The file *MSP430\Code43olite.fth* contains all the code definitions needed for a small standalone Forth kernel. Such a kernel is practical for the MSP430G2553 that has enough Flash and RAM. See *liteLP2553sa.ctl* for the control file.

If you are using Umbilical Forth, treat *MSP430\Code430olite.fth* as a source repository from which you can copy required words.

4.1 Register usage

On the MSP430 the following register usage is the default:

Forth	MSP430	Comments
IP	R1/SP	MSP430 PC
RSP		MSP430 return stack
--	R2/CG1/SR	
--	R3/CG2	
PSP	R4	data stack pointer
TOS	R5	cached top of data stack
UP	R6	USER area pointer
LP (locals)	R7	points to LOCALs on r. stack scratch
R8..R13		with R5 forms working stack codegen
R14		code generator temporary codegen
R15		preserves SR in shuffle

The VFX code generator reserves R14 and R15 for internal operations. CODE definitions must use R5 as TOS with NOS pointed to by R4 as a descending stack. R8..R15 are free for use by CODE definitions and need not be preserved or restored. You should assume that any register can be affected by other words.

4.2 Literal and flow of control

code execute   \ xt --
Execute the code described by the XT. This is a Forth equivalent to an assembler JSR/CALL instruction.

proc docreate   \ -- a-addr
The run time action of CREATE.

CODE (DO)   \ limit start --

The run time action of DO compiled on the target.

CODE (?DO) \ **limit start --**
The run time action of ?DO compiled on the target.

CODE (LOOP) \ -- ; absolute address follows inline
The run time action of LOOP compiled on the target.

CODE (+LOOP) \ **n --**
The run time action of +LOOP compiled on the target.

code i \ **-- n ; return DO ... LOOP index**
Return the current index of the inner-most DO..LOOP.

code j \ **-- n ; return outer DO ... LOOP index**
Return the current index of the outer DO..LOOP.

code unloop \ **-- ; discard DO ... LOOP parameters ; ANS 6.1.2380**
Remove the DO..LOOP control parameters from the return stack.

CODE LEAVE \ **-- ; leave DO ... LOOP**
Remove the current DO..LOOP parameters and jump to the end of the DO..LOOP structure.

4.3 Flash operations

: FlErase \ **addr len --**
Erase the Flash sectors in the given range.

: c!f \ **b addr --**
Program any address, including Flash, with an 8 bit value.

: !f \ **w addr --**
Program any address, including Flash, with a 16 bit value.

4.4 Digits and strings

code DIGIT \ char base -- 0 | n true

If the ASCII value *char* can be treated as a digit for a number in the given *base* then return the digit and a TRUE flag, otherwise just return FALSE. For bases greater than 10, the letters A..Z are used, e.g. 0..9,A..F for hexadecimal.

: /string \ addr len n -- addr+n len-n

Modify a string address and length to remove the first N characters from the string.

CODE CMOVE \ source dest len -- ; copy memory areas

Copy U bytes of memory forwards from C-ADDR1 to C-ADDR2.

CODE CMOVE> \ source dest len -- ; copy memory areas

As CMOVE but working in the opposite direction, copying the last character in the string first.

code fill \ addr len char --

Fill *len* bytes of memory starting at *addr* with the byte specified as *char*.

: ERASE \ addr len --

Fill *len* bytes of memory starting at *addr* with zero.

code s= \ addr1 addr2 count -- flag

Compare two same-length strings/memory blocks, returning TRUE if they are identical.

code SKIP \ c-addr u char -- 'c-addr 'u

Modify the string description by skipping over leading occurrences of 'char'.

code scan \ caddr u char -- caddr2 u2

Look for first occurrence of CHAR in string and return new string. C-addr2/u2 describe the string with CHAR as the first character.

: count \ addr -- addr+1 len

Given the address of a counted string in memory this word will return the address of the first character and the length in characters of the string.

: (")   \ -- addr ; in-line string follows caller, and skip it
Return the address of a counted string that is inline after the CALLING word,
and adjust the CALLING word's return address to step over the inline string.
See the definition of (.") for an example.

: upc   \ char -- char' ; force upper case
Convert char to upper case.

: upper   \ c-addr len --
Convert the ASCII string described to upper-case. This operation happens in place.

: PLACE   \ c-addr1 u c-addr2 --
Place the string c-addr1/u as a counted string at c-addr2.

4.5 Arithmetic

4.5.1 Basics

: 1+ 1+ ;   \ n -- n+1
Add one to top-of stack.

: 2+ 2+ ;   \ n -- n+2
Add two to top-of stack.

: 1- 1- ;   \ n -- n-1
Subtract one from top-of stack.

: 2- 2- ;   \ n -- n-2
Subtract two from top-of stack.

: 2* 2* ;   \ n1 -- n2
Signed multiply top of stack by 2.

: u2/ u2/ ;   \ n1 -- n2 ; unsigned
Unsigned divide top of stack by 2.

: 2/ 2/ ;   \ n1 -- n2 ; signed
Signed divide top of stack by 2.

: - - ;   \ n1 n2 -- n1-n2

Subtract two single precision integer numbers. N3|u3=n1|u1-n2|u2.

: + + ;   \ n1 n2 n1+n2

Add two single precision integer numbers.

: negate   \ n1 -- -n1

Negate a single precision integer number.

: abs   \ n1 -- |n1|

If n is negative, return its positive equivalent (absolute value).

: dnegate   \ d1 -- -d1

Negate a double number.

: dabs   \ d1 -- |d1|

If d is negative, return its positive equivalent (absolute value).

CODE D+   \ d1 d2 -- d3

Add two double precision integers.

CODE D-   \ d1 d2 -- d1-d2

Subtract two double precision integers. D3=D1-D2.

CODE S>D   \ n -- d

Convert a single number to a double one.

: D<   \ d1 d2 -- t/f

Return TRUE if the double number d1 is < the double number d2.

: d>   \ d1 d2 -- t/f

Return TRUE if the double number d1 is > the double number d2.

: d0=   \ d -- t/f

Returns true if d is 0.

: d=   \ d1 d2 -- t/f

Return TRUE if the two double numbers are equal.

4.5.2 Multiplication

code um*   \ u1 u2 -- ud ; unsigned multiply
Perform unsigned-multiply between two numbers and return double result.

code *   \ n1 n2 -- n1*n2 ; signed multiply, : * um* drop ;
Standard signed multiply. N3 = n1 * n2.

code m*   \ n1 n2 -- d ; signed multiply
Signed multiply yielding double result.

4.5.3 Division

code um/mod   \ u32 u16 -- urem uquot
Perform unsigned division of double number UD by single number U
and return remainder and quotient.

code sm/rem   \ d n -- rem quot ; symmetric division
Perform a signed division of double number D1 by single number N2
and return remainder and quotient using symmetric (normal) division.

: /mod   \ n1 n2 -- rem quot
Signed division of N1 by N2 single-precision yielding remainder and quotient.

: /   \ n1 n2 -- quot
Standard signed division operator. n3 = n1/n2.

: mod   \ n1 n2 -- rem
Return remainder of division of N1 by N2. n3 = n1 mod n2.

: MU/MOD   \ ud1 u2 -- u3 ud4
Perform an unsigned divide of a double ud1 by a single u2,
returning a single remainder u3 and a double quotient ud4.

4.6 Logic

: AND AND ;   \ n1 n2 -- n3
Perform a logical AND between the top two stack items

and retain the result in top of stack.

: OR OR ;   \ n1 n2 -- n3
Perform a logical OR between the top two stack items
and retain the result in top of stack.

: XOR XOR ;   \ n1 n2 -- n3
Perform a logical XOR between the top two stack items
and retain the result in top of stack.

: INVERT INVERT ;   \ n1 -- n2
Perform a bitwise NOT on the top stack item and retain result.

4.7 Shifts

code lshift   \ x count -- x'
Left shift x by count bits.

code rshift   \ x count -- x'
Right shift x by count bits.

4.8 Return stack words

CODE >R   \ x -- ; R: -- x
Push the current top item of the data stack onto the top of the return stack.

CODE R@   \ -- x ; R: x -- x
Copy the top item from the return stack to the data stack.

CODE R>   \ -- x ; R: x --
Pop the top item from the return stack to the data stack.

4.9 Comparisons

: =   \ n1 n2 -- flag
Return TRUE if the two topmost stack items are equal.

: <>   \ n1 n2 -- flag
Return TRUE if the two topmost stack items are different.

: 0<>   \ n -- **flag**
    Compare the top stack item with 0 and return TRUE if not-equal.

: 0=   \ n -- **flag**
    Compare the top stack item with 0 and return TRUE if equals.

: 0<   \ n -- **flag**
    Return TRUE if the top of stack is less-than-zero.

: 0>   \ n -- **flag**
    Return TRUE if the top of stack is greater-than-zero.

: U<   \ n1 n2 -- **flag**
    An UNSIGNED version of <.

: U>   \ n1 n2 -- **flag**
    An UNSIGNED version of >.

: <   \ n1 n2 -- **t/f**
    Return TRUE if n1 is less than n2.

: >   \ n1 n2 -- **t/f**
    Return TRUE if n1 is greater than n2.

: <=   \ n1 n2 -- **t/f**
    Return TRUE if n1 is less than or equal to n2.

: >=   \ n1 n2 -- **t/f**
    Return TRUE if n1 is greater than or equal to n2.

4.10 Stack primitives

: OVER over ;   \ n1 n2 -- n1 n2 n1
    Copy NOS to a new top-of-stack item.

: 2OVER   \ n1 n2 n3 n4 -- n1 n2 n3 n4 n1 n2
    Similar to OVER but works with cell-pairs rather than cell items.

: DROP drop ;   \ n1 --
    Lose the top data stack item and promote NOS to TOS.

: 2DROP 2drop ;   \ n1 n2 --
    Discard the top two data stack items.

: SWAP swap ;   \ n1 n2 -- n2 n1
    Exchange the top two data stack items.

: 2SWAP   \ n1 n2 n3 n4 -- n3 n4 n1 n2
    Exchange the top two cell-pairs on the data stack.

: DUP dup ;   \ n1 -- n1 n1
    DUPlicate the top stack item.

: 2DUP 2dup ;   \ n1 n2 -- n1 n2 n1 n2
    DUPlicate the top cell-pair on the data stack.

: ?dup   \ n1 -- n1 [n1]
    DUPlicate the top stack item only if it non-zero.

: nip nip ;   \ n1 n2 -- n2
    Dispose of the second item on the data stack.

: tuck   \ n1 n2 -- n2 n1 n2
    Insert a copy of the top data stack item underneath the current second item.

: pick   \ nn..n0 n -- nn..n0 nn
    Get a copy of the Nth data stack item and place on top of stack.
    0PICK is equivalent to DUP.

: ROT   \ n1 n2 n3 -- n2 n3 n1
    ROTate the positions of the top three stack items such that
    the current top of stack becomes the second item. See also ROLL.

: -rot   \ n1 n2 n3 -- n3 n1 n2
    The inverse of ROT.

: C@ c@ ;   \ addr -- b
    Fetch and 0 extend the character at memory ADDR and return.

: @ @ ;   \ addr -- n
     Fetch and return the CELL at memory ADDR.

: 2@ 2@ ;   \ addr -- d
     Fetch and return the two CELLS from memory ADDR and ADDR+sizeof(CELL).
     The cell at the lower address is on the top of the stack.

: C!   \ b addr --
     Store the character CHAR at memory C-ADDR.

: !   \ n addr --
     Store the CELL quantity N at memory ADDR.

: 2!   \ d addr --
     Store the two CELLS x1 and x2 at memory ADDR. X2 is stored
     at ADDR and X1 is stored at ADDR+CELL.

CODE +!   \ n addr --
     Add N to the CELL at memory address ADDR.**code noop** \ -- ; **dummy**
     A NOOP, null instruction.)

: within   \ n1|u1 n2|u2 n3|u3 -- flag ; ANS 6.2.2440
     The ANS version of WITHIN?. This word uses unsigned arithmetic,
     so that signed compares are treated as existing on a number circle.

: on   \ addr --
     Given the address of a CELL this will set its contents to TRUE (-1).

: off   \ addr --
     Given the address of a CELL this will set its contents to FALSE (0).

: bounds   \ addr len -- addr+len addr
     Convert an address and length to adress+length and address
     as required for DO..LOOP to use I as the current address.

: name>   \ nfa -- cfa ; convert name address to CFA
     Move a pointer from an NFA to the CFA or "XT" in ANS parlance.

: >name　　　　　　　　**\ cfa -- nfa**

Move a pointer from an XT back to the NFA or name-pointer.
If the original pointer was not an XT or if the definition in question
has no name header in the dictionary the returned pointer will be useless.
Care should be taken when manipulating or scanning the Forth dictionary
in this way.

: SEARCH-WORDLIST　　　　**\ c-addr u wid -- 0|xt 1|xt -1**

Search the given wordlist for a definition. If the definition is not found then
0 is returned, otherwise the XT of the definition is returned along with a
non-zero code. A -ve code indicates a normal definition and a +ve code
indicates an IMMEDIATE word.

4.11 Portability words

Using these words will make code easier to port between 16, 32 and 64 bit targets.

cell constant cell　　　　　**\ -- 2**

Return the size in address units of one CELL.

: cells　　　　　　　　　**\ n -- n*2**

Return the number of bytes required to hold the given number of 16 bit cells.

: aligned　　　　　　　　**\ addr -- addr'**

Given an address pointer this word will return the next aligned address subject
to system wide alignment restrictions.

: >body　　　　　**\ xt -- pfa ; step from code field to parameter field**

Move a pointer from a CFA or "XT" to the definition BODY. This should only
be used with children of CREATE. E.g. if FOOBAR is defined with
CREATEfoobar, then the phrase 'foobar >body would yield the same result
as executing foobar.

: compile,　　　　　　　　**\ addr --**

Compile the word specified by xt into the current definition.

4.12 Defining words

: DOES>   \ C: colon-sys1 -- colon-sys2 ; Run: -- ; R: nest-sys --
Begin definition of the runtime action of a child of a defining word.
You should not use RECURSE after DOES>.

: :   \ C: "<spaces>name" -- colon-sys ; Exec: i*x -- j*x ; R: -- nest-sys
Begin a new definition called name.

: CONSTANT   \ x "<spaces>name" -- ; Exec: -- x
Create a new CONSTANT called name which has the value "x".
When NAME executes the value *\i{x) is returned.

: EQU   \ x "<spaces>name" -- ; Exec: -- x
A synonym for CONSTANT abve to ease interactive debugging of target
drivers that are normally cross-compiled. Create a new CONSTANT called
name which has the value "x". When NAME executes the value *\i{x) is
returned.

: VARIABLE   \ "<spaces>name" -- ; Exec: -- a-addr
Create a new variable called name. When Name is executed the address
of the RAM is returned for use with @ and !. The RAM is not initialised.

: USER   \ u "<spaces>name" -- ; Exec: -- addr
Create a new USER variable called name. The 'u' parameter specifies the
index into the user-area table at which to place the data. USER variables are
located in a separate area of memory for each task or interrupt. Use in the
form:

    $400 USER TaskData

: DEFER   \ Comp: "<spaces>name" -- ; Run: i*x -- j*x
Creates a new DEFERed word. No default action is assigned. User-defined
DEFERed words must be initialised by the application before use.

   ' <action> IS <deferredword>

or (when compiled)

    ['] <action> IS <deferredword>

4.13 Miscellaneous

defer pause   \ -- ; multitasker hook
    Allows the sytem multitasker to get a look in.
    If the multitasker has not been compiled, PAUSE is set to NOOP.

code reboot   \ --
    Starts the watchdog and waits until the CPU reboots.

: bor!   \ mask addr --
    Set *mask* bits in the byte at *addr*.

: bbic!   \ mask addr --
    Clear *mask* bits in the byte at *addr*.

: btoggle!   \ mask addr --
    Toggle the *mask* bits in the byte at *addr*.

: btst   \ mask addr -- x
    Return non-zero if the *mask* bits in the byte at *addr* are non-zero.

: or!   \ mask addr --
    Set *mask* bits in the word/cell at *addr*.

: bic!   \ mask addr --
    Clear *mask* bits in the word/cell at *addr*.

: toggle!   \ mask addr --
    Toggle the *mask* bits in the word/cell at *addr*.

: tst   \ mask addr -- x
    Return non-zero if the *mask* bits in the word/cell at *addr* are non-zero.

5 High level kernel - kernel72lite.fth.

The Forth kernel words documented here are entirely written in high-level Forth. The kernel is reduced in size to match available code size in small devices such as the MSP430G2553 in the TI Launchpad.

5.1 User variables

variable next-user   \ -- addr
Next valid offset for a USER variable created by +USER.

: +user   \ size --
Used in the cross compiler to create a USER variable *size* bytes long at the next available offset and updates that offset.

tcb-size +user SELF   \ task identifier and TCB
When multitasking is installed, the task control block for a task occupies TCB-SIZE bytes at the start of the user area.
Thus the user area pointer also acts as a pointer to the task control block.

cell +user S0   \ base of data stack
Holds the initial setting of the data stack pointer.
N.B. S0, R0, #TIB and 'TIB must be defined in that order.

cell +user R0   \ base of return stack
Holds the initial setting of the return stack pointer.

cell +user #TIB   \ number of chars currently in TIB
Holds the number of characters currently in TIB.

cell +user 'TIB   \ address of TIB
Holds the address of TIB, the terminal input buffer.

cell +user >IN   \ offset into TIB
Holds the current character position being processed in the input stream.

cell +user OUT   \ number of chars displayed on current line
Holds the number of chars displayed on current output line. Reset by CR.

cell +user DPL \ **position of double number character id**
Holds the number of characters after the double number indicator character.
DPL is initialised to -1, which indicates a single number, and is incremented for
each character after the separator.

cell +user OPVEC \ **output vector**
Holds the address of the I/O vector for the current output device.

cell +user IPVEC \ **input vector**
Holds the address of the I/O vector for the current input device.

#64 chars dup +user PAD
A temporary string scratch buffer.

5.2 System data

5.2.1 Constants

$20 constant BL \ -- **char**
A blank space character.

5.2.2 System variables and data
Note that FENCE, DP, RP and VOC-LINK must be declared in that order.

variable DP \ -- **addr**
Flash dictionary pointer.

variable RP \ -- **addr**
RAM dictionary pointer.

variable xDP DP xDP ! \ -- **addr**
Holds the address of the current dictionary pointer, DP or RP.

variable LAST \ -- **addr**
Points to name field of last definition

5.3 Vectored I/O handling

5.3.1 Introduction

The standard console Forth I/O words (KEY?, KEY, EMIT, TYPE and CR) can be used with any I/O device by placing the address of a table of xts in the USER variables IPVEC and OPVEC. IPVEC (input vector) controls the actions of KEY? and KEY, and OPVEC(output vector) controls the actions of EMIT, TYPE and CR. Adding a new device is matter of writing the five primitives, building the table, and storing the address of the table in the pointers IPVEC and OPVEC to make the new device active. Any initialisation must be performed before the device is made active.

Note that for the output words (EMIT, TYPE and CR) the USER variable OUT is handled in the kernel before the funtion in the table is called.

5.3.2 Building a vector table
The example below is taken from an ARM implementation.

create Console1	\ -- addr
' serkey1i ,	\ -- char
' serkey?1i ,	\ -- flag
' seremit1 ,	\ char --
' sertype1 ,	\ c-addr len --
' serCR1 ,	\ --

Console1 opvec !   Console1 ipvec !

5.3.3 Generic I/O words

: key   \ -- char ; receive char
Wait until the current input device receives a character and return it.

: KEY?   \ -- flag ; check receive char

Return true if a character is available at the current input device.

: EMIT   \ -- char ; display char
Display char on the current I/O device. OUT is incremented
before executing the vector function.

: TYPE   \ caddr len -- ; display string
Display/write the string on the current output device.
Len is added to OUT before executing the vector function.

: CR   \ -- ; display new line
Perform the equivalent of a CR/LF pair on the current output device.
OUT is zeroed. before executing the vector function.

: SPACE   \ --
Output a blank space (ASCII 32) character.

: SPACES   \ n --
Output *n* spaces, where *n* > 0. If *n* < 0, no action is taken.

5.4 Laying data in memory

These words are used to control and place data in memory. Note that the Forth system
compiles headers and code into Flash memory.

: HERE   \ -- addr
Return the current dictionary pointer which is the first address-unit
of free space within the system.

: ORG   \ addr --
Set the current dictionary pointer.

: ALLOT   \ n --
Allocate N address-units of data space from the current value of HERE
and move the pointer.

: RHERE   \ -- addr
Return the current RAM dictionary pointer.

: RALLOT   \ n --
Allocate n bytes of RAM from RHERE and move the pointer.

: ROM   \ --

    HERE, ORG, ALLOT, , and friends, are set to use the Flash dictionary pointer.
    This is the default.

: RAM   \ --

    HERE, ORG and ALLOT are set to use the RAM dictionary pointer. Use in the form:
    RAM ... ROM

: aligned   \ addr -- addr'

    Given an address pointer this word will return the next ALIGNED address
    subject to system wide alignment restrictions.

: ALIGN   \ --

    ALIGN dictionary pointer using the same rules as ALIGNED.

: ,   \ x --

    Place the CELL value X into the dictionary at HERE and increment the pointer.

: C,   \ char --

Place the CHAR value into the dictionary at HERE and increment the pointer.

5.5 Dictionary management

The Forth header is laid out as below. The start and end of the header are aligned at
cell boundaries.

Link	Count	<name>

Cell	Byte	n Bytes

Also called LFA. This field contains the address of the of the next count byte in the
same thread of the wordlist.
The bottom five bits contain the length (0..31) of the name in bytes. The top three Bits
are used as follows:

Count/Ctrl	
Bit 7	Always set
Bit 6	Immediate bit (0=immediate)
Bit 5	Reserved

\<name\>   A string of ASCII characters which make up the name of the word..

: FIND   \ c-addr -- c-addr 0|xt 1|xt -1

Perform the SEARCH-WORDLIST operation on all wordlists within the current search order. This definition takes a counted string rather than a *c-addr/u* pair. The counted string is returned as well as the 0 on failure.

: .NAME   \ nfa --

Display a definition's name given an NFA.

: CREATE   \ --

Create a new definition in the dictionary. When the new definition is executed it will return the address of the definition's data area. As compilation is into Flash, CREATE cannot be used with DOES> and <BUILDS...DOES>... must be used instead.

: <BUILDS   \ --

Always used in the form:

: defword <BUILDS ... DOES> ... ;

When defword is executed a new definition is created with the data defined between <BUILDS and DOES> and the action defined between DOES> and ;. You must use <BUILDS and DOES> together, otherwise there will be a crash. Treat <BUILDS as a special case of CREATE for use with DOES> and compilation into Flash.

5.6 String compilation

: (C")   \ -- c-addr

The run-time action for C" which returns the address of and steps over a counted string. INTERNAL.

: (S")   \ -- c-addr u

The run-time action for S" which returns the address and length of and steps over a string. INTERNAL.

: (ABORT")   \ i*x x1 -- | i*x

The run time action of ABORT". INTERNAL.

: (.")   \ --
    The run-time action of .". INTERNAL.

5.7 ANS words CATCH and THROW

CATCH and THROW form the basis of all Forth error handling. The following description of CATCH and THROW originates with Mitch Bradley and is taken from an ANS Forth standard draft.

CATCH and THROW provide a reliable mechanism for handling exceptions, without having to propagate exception flags through multiple levels of word nesting. It is similar in spirit to the "nonlocal return" mechanisms of many other languages, such as C's setjmp() and longjmp(), and LISP's CATCH and THROW. In the Forth context, THROW may be described as a "multi-level EXIT", with CATCH marking a location to which a THROW may return.

Several similar Forth "multi-level EXIT" exception-handling schemes have been described and used in past years. It is not possible to implement such a scheme using only standard words (other than CATCH and THROW), because there is no portable way to "unwind" the return stack to a predetermined place.
THROW also provides a convenient implementation technique for the standard words ABORT and ABORT", allowing an application to define, through the use of CATCH, the behavior in the event of a system abort.

5.7.1 Example use

If THROW is executed with a non zero argument, the effect is as if the corresponding CATCH had returned it. In that case, the stack depth is the same as it was just before CATCH began execution. The values of the i*x stack arguments could have been modified arbitrarily during the execution of xt. In general, nothing useful may be done with those stack items, but since their number is known (because the stack depth is deterministic), the application may DROP them to return to a predictable stack state.

Typical use:

: could-fail	\ -- char
KEY DUP [CHAR] Q =	
IF 1 THROW THEN	

;	

: do-it	\ a b - - c
DROP could-fail	
;	

: try-it	\ - -
1 2 ['] do-it CATCH IF	
(-- x1 x2) 2DROP ." There was an exception" CR	
ELSE	
." The character was " EMIT CR	
THEN	
;	

: retry-it	\ - -
1 2 ['] do-it CATCH IF	
WHILE	
(-- x1 x2) 2DROP ." Exception, keep trying" CR	
REPEAT (char)	
." The character was " EMIT CR	
;	

5.7.2 Gotchas

If a THROW is performed without a CATCH in place, the system will/may crash.
As the current exception frame is pointed to by the USER variable HANDLER, each
task and interrupt handler will need a CATCH if THROW is used inside it.
You can no longer use ABORT as a way of resetting the data stack and calling QUIT.
ABORT is now defined as -1THROW.

5.7.3 User words

: CATCH   \ i*x xt -- j*x 0|i*x n

   Execute the code at XT with an exception frame protecting it. CATCH returns a 0
   if no error has occurred, otherwise it returns the throw-code passed to the last
   THROW.

: THROW   \ **k*x n -- k*x|i*x n**

    Throw a non-zero exception code n back to the last CATCH call. If n is 0, no action
    is taken except to DROP n.

: ?throw   \ **flag throw-code -- ; SFP017**

    Perform a THROW of value throw-code if flag is non-zero, otherwise
    do nothing except discard flag and throw-code.

: ABORT"   \ **Comp: "ccc<quote>" -- ; Run: i*x x1 -- | i*x ; R: j*x -- | j*x**

    If x1 is non-zero at run-time, store the address of the following counted string
    in USER variable 'ABORTTEXT, and perform -2THROW.
    The text interpreter in QUIT will (if reached) display the text.

5.8 Formatted and unformatted i/o

5.8.1 Setting number bases

: HEX   \ **--**

    Change current radix to base 16.

: DECIMAL   \ **--**

    Change current radix to base 10.

: BIN   \ **--**

    Change current radix to base 2.

5.8.2 Numeric output

: HOLD   \ **char --**

    Insert the ASCII 'char' value into the pictured numeric output string
    currently being assembled.

: #   \ **ud1 -- ud2**

    Given a double number on the stack this will add the next digit to the pictured
    numeric output buffer and return the next double number to work with.
    PLEASE NOTE that the numeric output string is built from right (l.s. digit) to

left (m.s. digit).

: #S \ ud1 -- ud2

Keep performing # until all digits are generated.

: <# \ --

Begin definition of a new numeric output string buffer.

: #> \ xd -- c-addr u

Terminate defnition of a numeric output string.
Return the address and length of the ASCII string.

: D.R \ d n --

Output the double number 'd' using current radix, right justified to 'n' characters.
Padding is inserted using spaces on the left side.

: D. \ d --

Output the double number 'd' without padding.

: . \ n --

Output the cell signed value 'n' without justification.

: U. \ u --

As with . but treat as unsigned.

: .R \ n1 n2 --

As D.R but uses a single-signed cell value.

5.8.3 Numeric input

: +DIGIT \ d1 n -- d2 ;

accumulates digit into double accumulator Multiply d1 by the current radix
and add n to it. INTERNAL.

: >NUMBER \ ud1 c-addr1 u1 -- ud2 c-addr2 u2 ; convert all until non-digits

Accumulate digits from string c-addr1/u2 into double number ud1 to produce
ud2 until the first non-convertible character is found. c-addr2/u2 represents
the remaining string with caddr2 pointing the non-convertible character. The
number base for conversion is defined by the contents of USER variable BASE.

>NUMBER is case insensitive.

: (INTEGER?)   \ c-addr u -- d/n/- 2/1/0
The guts of INTEGER? but without the base override handling. See INTEGER?
INTERNAL.

: Check-Prefix   \ addr len -- addr' len'
If any BASE override prefices or suffices are used in the input string,
set BASE accordingly and return the string without the override
characters. INTERNAL.

: number?   \ $addr -- n 1 | d 2 | 0
Attempt to convert the counted string at 'addr' to an integer. The return result
is either 0 for failed, 1 for a single-cell return result followed by that cell, or 2
for a double return. The ASCII number string supplied can also contain
implicit radix over-rides. A leading $ enforces hexadecimal, a leading #
enforces decimal and a leading % enforces binary.

5.9 String input and output

: BS   \ -- ; destructive backspace
Perform a destructive backspace by issuing ASCII characters 8, 20h, 8. If OUT is
non-zero at the start, it is decremented by one regardless of the actions of the
device driver. INTERNAL.

: ?BS   \ pos -- pos' step ; perform BS if pos non-zero
If pos is non-zero and ECHOING is set, perform BS and return the size of the step,
0 or -1. INTERNAL.

: SAVE-CH   \ char addr -- ; save as required
Save char at addr, and output the character if ECHOING is set. INTERNAL.

: ."   \ "ccc<quote>" --
Output the text upto the closing double-quotes character. Use .(<text>)
when interpreting.

: $.   \ c-addr -- ; display counted string
Output a counted-string to the output device.

: ACCEPT   \ c-addr +n1 -- +n2 ; read up to LEN chars into ADDR
Read a string of maximum size n1 characters to the buffer at c-addr, returning
n2 the number of characters actually read. Input may be terminated by CR.
The action may be input device specific. If ECHOING is non-zero, characters
are echoed. If XON/XOFF is non-zero, an XON character is sent at the start
and an XOFF character is sent at the the the end.

5.10 Source input control

: SOURCE-ID   \ -- n ; indicates input source
Returns an indicator of which device is generating source input. See the ANS
specification for more details.

: SOURCE   \ -- c-addr u
Returns the address and length of the current terminal input buffer. INTERNAL

: QUERY   \ -- ; fetch line into TIB
Reset the input source specification to the console and accept a line of text into the
input buffer.

5.11 Text scanning

: PARSE   \ char "ccc<char>" -- c-addr u
Parse the next token from the terminal input buffer using <char> as the
delimiter. The next token is returned as a c-addr/u string description. Note
that PARSE does not skip leading delimiters. If you need to skip leading
delimiters, use PARSE-WORD instead.

: PARSE-WORD   \ char -- c-addr u ; find token, skip leading chars
An alternative to WORD below. The return is a *c-addr/u* pair rather than a counted
string and no copy has occured, i.e. the contents of HERE are unaffected. Because
no intermediate global buffers are used PARSE-WORD is more reliable than
WORD for text scanning in multi-threaded applications. INTERNAL.

: WORD   \ char "<chars>ccc<char>" -- c-addr
Similar behaviour to the ANS word PARSE but the returned string is described as a
counted string.

5.12 Miscellaneous

: WORDS   \ --

Display the names of all definitions in the wordlist at the top of the search-order.

: MOVE   \ addr1 addr2 u -- ; intelligent move

An intelligent memory move, chooses between CMOVE and CMOVE> at runtime to avoid memory overlap problems. Note that as ROM PowerForth characters are 8 bit, there is an implicit connection between a byte and a character.

: DEPTH   \ ??? -- +n

Return the number of items on the data stack.

: .FREE   \ --

Return the free dictionary space.

5.13 Wordlist control

here is-action-of vocabulary \ -The runtime action of a VOCABULARY.

5.14 Control structures

: ?PAIRS   \ x1 x2 --

If x1<>x2, issue and error. Used for on-target compile-time error checking. INTERNAL.

: !CSP   \ x --

Save the stack pointer in CSP. Used for on-target compile-time error checking. INTERNAL.

: ?CSP   \ --

Issue an error if the stack pointer is not the same as the value previously stored in CSP. Used for on-target compile-time error checking. INTERNAL.

: ?COMP   \ --

Error if not in compile state. INTERNAL.

: ?EXEC \ --
Error if not interpreting. INTERNAL.

: DO \ C: -- do-sys ; Run: n1|u1 n2|u2 -- ; R: -- loop-sys
Begin a DO...LOOP construct. Takes the end-value and start-value
from the data-stack.

: ?DO \ C: -- do-sys ; Run: n1|u1 n2|u2 -- ; R: -- | loop-sys
Compile a DO which will only begin loop execution if the loop parameters are not
the same. Thus 00?DO...LOOP will not execute the contents of the loop.

: LOOP \ C: do-sys -- ; Run: -- ; R: loop-sys1 -- | loop-sys2
The closing statement of a DO..LOOP construct. Increments the index
and terminates when the index crosses the limit.

: +LOOP \ C: do-sys -- ; Run: n -- ; R: loop-sys1 -- | loop-sys2
As with LOOP except that you specify the increment on the data-stack.

: BEGIN \ C: -- dest ; Run: --
Mark the start of a structure of the form:
  BEGIN ... [WHILE] ... UNTIL / AGAIN / [REPEAT]

: AGAIN \ C: dest -- ; Run: --
The end of a BEGIN..AGAIN construct which specifies an infinite loop.)

: UNTIL \ C: dest -- ; Run: x --
Compile code into definition which will jump back to the matching BEGIN if the
supplied condition flag is Zero/FALSE.

: WHILE \ C: dest -- orig dest ; Run: x --
Separate the condition test from the loop code in a BEGIN..WHILE..REPEAT block.

: REPEAT \ C: orig dest -- ; Run: --
Loop back to the conditional dest code in a BEGIN..WHILE..REPEAT construct.)

: IF \ C: -- orig ; Run: x --
Mark the start of an IF..[ELSE]..THEN conditional block.

: THEN \ C: orig -- ; Run: --
Mark the end of an IF..THEN or IF..ELSE..THEN conditional construct.

: ELSE   \ C: orig1 -- orig2 ; Run: --
    Begin the failure condition code for an IF.

: RECURSE   \ Comp: --
    Compile a recursive call to the colon definition containing RECURSE itself.
    Do not use RECURSE between DOES> and ;. Used in the form:

: foo ... recurse ... ;
    to compile a reference to FOO from inside FOO.

5.15 Target interpreter and compiler

: ?STACK   \ --
    Error if stack pointer out of range. INTERNAL.

: ?UNDEF   \ x --
    Word not defined error if x=0. INTERNAL.

: POSTPONE   \ Comp: "<spaces>name" --
    Compile a reference to another word. POSTPONE can handle compilation
    of IMMEDIATE words which would otherwise be executed during compilation.

: S"   \ Comp: "ccc<quote>" -- ; Run: -- c-addr u
    Describe a string. Text is taken up to the next double-quote character.
    The address and length of the string are returned.

: C"   \ Comp: "ccc<quote>" -- ; Run: -- c-addr
    As S" except the address of a counted string is returned.

: LITERAL   \ Comp: x -- ; Run: -- x
    Compile a literal into the current definition. Usually used in the form
    [<expression]LITERAL inside a colon definition. Note that LITERAL
    is IMMEDIATE.

: CHAR   \ "<spaces>name" -- char
    Return the first character of the next token in the input stream.
    Usually used to avoid magic numbers in the source code.

: [CHAR]   \ Comp: "<spaces>name" -- ; Run: -- char
Compile the first character of the next token in the input stream as a literal.
Usually used to avoid magic numbers in the source code.

: [\ --
Switch compiler into interpreter state.

:]   \ --
Switch compiler into compilation state.

: IMMEDIATE   \ --
Mark the last defined word as IMMEDIATE. Immediate words will execute
whenever encountered regardless of STATE.

: '   \ "<spaces>name" -- xt
Find the xt of the next word in the input stream. An error occurs if the xt cannot
be found.

: [']   \ Comp: "<spaces>name" -- ; Run: -- xt
Find the xt of the next word in the input stream, and compile it as a literal.
An error occurs if the xt cannot be found.

: [COMPILE]   \ "<spaces>name" --
Compile the next word in the input stream. [COMPILE] ignores
the IMMEDIATE state of the word.
[COMPILE] is mostly superceded by POSTPONE.

: (\ "ccc<paren>" --
Begin an inline comment. All text upto the closing bracket is ignored.

**: **   \ "ccc<eol>" --
Begin a single-line comment. All text up to the end of the line is ignored.

: ",   \ "ccc<quote>" --
Parse text up to the closing quote and compile into the dictionary at HERE as a
counted string. The end of the string is aligned.

: (TO-DO)   \ -- ; R: xt -- a-addr'
The run-time action of IS. It is followed by the data addres of the DEFERred word

at which the xt is stored. INTERNAL.

: IS   \ **"<spaces>name" --**

The second part of the ASSIGNxxxTO-DOyyy construct. This word will assign the given XT to be the action of a DEFERed word which is named in the input stream.

: exit   \ **R: nest-sys -- ; exit current definition**

Compile code into the current definition to cause a definition to terminate. This is the Forth equivalent to inserting an RTS/RET instruction in the middle of an assembler subroutine.

: ;   \ **C: colon-sys -- ; Run: -- ; R: nest-sys --**

Complete the definition of a new 'colon' word or :NONAME code block.

: INTERPRET   \ **--**

Process the current input line as if it is text entered at the keyboard.

: EVALUATE   \ **i*x c-addr u -- j*x ; interpret the string**

Process the supplied string as though it had been entered via the interpreter.

: .throw   \ **throw# --**

Display the throw code. Values of 0 and –1 are ignored.

: QUIT   \ **-- ; R: i*x --**

Empty the return stack, store 0 in SOURCE-ID, and enter interpretation state. QUIT repeatedly ACCEPTs a line of input and INTERPRETs it, with a prompt if interpreting and ECHOING is on. Note that any task that uses QUIT must initialise 'TIB, BASE, IPVEC, and OPVEC.

5.16 Startup code

5.16.1 The COLD sequence

At power up, the target executes COLD or the word specified by MAKE-TURNKEY<name>, or the word specified as the action of an application compiled by the target.

: (INIT)   \ --
Performs the high level Forth startup. See the source code for more details.
INTERNAL.

: Commit   \ xt|0 --
Preserve the compiled image. If xt is non-zero, that word will be executed when
the application starts.

: Empty   \ --
Wipe the application and perform a cold restart.

: COLD   \ --
The first high level word executed by default. This word is set to be the word
executed at power up, but this may be overridden by a later use of MAKE-
TURNKEY<name> in the cross-compiled code. See the source code for more
details of COLD.

5.17 Kernel error codes

-1	ABORT
-2	ABORT
-4	Stack underflow
-13	Undefined word.
-14	Attempt to interpret a compile only definition.
-22	Control structure mismatch - unbalanced control structure.
-121	Attempt to remove with MARKER or FORGET below FENCE in protected dictionary.
-403	Attempt to compile an interpret only definition.
-501	Error if not LOADing from a block.

6 Time Delays

The code in *Delays.fth* allows you to handle time delays specified in milliseconds.

: ticks   (-- n) <ticks> @ ;
Return current clock value in milliseconds. This value can treated as a 16 bit unsigned value that wraps when it overflows.

: later   \ n -- n'
Generates the timebase value for termination in n millseconds time.

: timedout?   \ n -- flag ; true if timed out
Flag is returned true if the timebase value n has timed out. TIMEDOUT? does not call PAUSE.

: ms   \ n --
Waits for n milliseconds.

7   Debug tools

Some simple debug tools can be found in *dump.fth*.

: dump   \ addr len --
Display the given block of memory.

: .S   \ i*x -- i*x
Display the stack contents

8   Compile source code from AIDE

The file *include.fth* provides support for compiling a source file from the AIDE server.

: end-load   \ -- ; switch back to keyboard input
This word is automatically performed at the end of a download to tidy up the comms.

: file-error   \ n --
Handle an error when a file is being INCLUDEd.

: $include   \ $addr -- ; compile host file, counted string

Given a counted string representing a file name, compile the file from AIDE.

: include   **\ "<filename>" -- ; load file from host**

Compile a file across the serial line from the AIDE file server. Use in the form:
include <filename>

The filename extension must be supplied.

9 Minimal Umbilical code definitions

The file *Min430.fth* contains the minimum code definitions required to support Umbilical Forth. If additional definitions are required, they may be copied to a new file from *Code430lite.fth* or *kernel72lite.fth*.

Note that many of the words documented here are only included by the early non-optimising compiler. These words will be removed from this file in a future release. If needed, they may then be copied from another file.

9.1 Logical and relational operators

: min   \ n1 n2 -- min(n1,n2)

Given two data stack items preserve only the smaller.

: max   \ n1 n2 -- max(n1,n2)

Given two data stack items preserve only the larger.

code within?   \ x a b -- t/f ; true if a<=x<=b

Return TRUE if N1 is within the range N2..N3. This word uses signed arithmetic.

code within   \ n1|u1 n2|u2 n3|u3 -- flag ; ANS 6.2.2440

The ANS version of WITHIN?. Return TRUE if N1 is within the range N2..N3-1. This word uses unsigned arithmetic, so that signed compares are treated as existing on a number circle.

9.2 Control flow

CODE (DO)   \ limit start --

The run time action of DO compiled on the target.

CODE (?DO)   \ limit start --

The run time action of ?DO compiled on the target.

CODE (LOOP)   \ -- ; absolute address follows inline

The run time action of LOOP compiled on the target.

CODE (+LOOP)   \ n --

The run time action of +LOOP compiled on the target.

code i   \ -- n ; return DO ... LOOP index

Return the current DO...LOOP index.

code j   \ -- n ; return DO ... LOOP index

Return the outer DO...LOOP index.

CODE EXECUTE   \ xt --

Execute the code described by the XT.

This is a Forth equivalent to an assembler JSR/CALL instruction.

Code Noop   \ -- ; used by multi-tasker

A NOOP, null instruction.)

CODE S>D   \ n -- d

Convert a single number to a double one.

code um*   \ u1 u2 -- ud ; unsigned multiply

Perform unsigned-multiply between two numbers and return double result.

code *   \ n1 n2 -- n1*n2 ; signed multiply, : * um* drop ;

Standard signed multiply. N3 = n1 * n2.

code m*   \ n1 n2 -- d ; signed multiply

Signed multiply yielding double result.

code um/mod   \ u32 u16 -- urem uquot

Perform unsigned division of double number UD by single number U and return remainder and quotient.

code sm/rem   \ d n -- rem quot ; symmetric division

Perform a signed division of double number D1 by single number N2 and return remainder and quotient using symmetric (normal) division.

code fm/mod   \ d n -- frem fquot ; floored division

Perform a signed division of double number D1 by single number N2 and return remainder and quotient using floored division. See the ANS Forth specification for more details of floored division.

: /mod   \ n1 n2 -- rem quot

Signed division of N1 by N2 single-precision yielding remainder and quotient.

: /   \ n1 n2 -- quot

Standard signed division operator. n3 = n1/n2.

: mod   \ n1 n2 -- rem

Return remainder of division of N1 by N2. n3 = n1 mod n2.

: MU/MOD   \ ud u -- urem udquot

Perform an unsigned divide of a double by a single, returning a single remainder and a double quotient.

: */MOD   \ n1 n2 n3 -- rem quot

Multiply n1 by n2 to give a double precision result, and then divide it by n3 returning the remainder and quotient. The point of this operation is to avoid loss of precision.

: */   \ n1 n2 n3 -- quot

Multiply n1 by n2 to give a double precision result, and then divide it by n3 returning the quotient. The point of this operation is to avoid loss of precision.

: M/   \ d n -- quot

Signed divide of a double by a single integer.

CODE negate   \ n1 -- -n1

Negate a single number.

: ?negate   \ n1 t/f -- n1/-n1

If flag is negative, then negate n1.

: abs   \ n1 -- |n1|

If n is negative, return its positive equivalent (absolute value).

code dnegate   \ d1 -- -d1

Negate a double number.

: ?dnegate   \ d1 t/f -- d1/-d1

If flag is negative, then negate d1.

CODE D+   \ d1 d2 -- d3

Add two double precision integers.

CODE D- \ d1 d2 -- d1-d2

Subtract two double precision integers. D3=D1-D2.

9.3 Stack manipulation

Many of the standard Forth stack manipulation words are just code generators in the cross compiler and have no target versions.

: ROLL \ n1 n2 .. nk n -- wierd

Rotate the order of the top N stack items by one place such that the current top of stack becomes the second item and the Nth item becomes TOS. See also ROT. N.B. Very slow.

The standard Forth comparison words words are just code generators in the cross compiler and have no target versions.

Some of the standard Forth memory manipulation words are just code generators in the cross compiler and have no target versions.

code c@ \ addr -- b

Fetch and 0 extend the character at memory ADDR and return.

code @ \ addr -- n

Fetch and return the CELL at memory ADDR.

code 2@ \ addr -- d

Fetch and return the two CELLS from memory ADDR and ADDR+sizeof(CELL). The cell at the lower address is on the top of the stack.

CODE C! \ b addr --

Store the character CHAR at memory C-ADDR.

CODE ! \ n addr --

Store the CELL quantity N at memory ADDR.

CODE 2! \ d addr --

Store the two CELLS x1 and x2 at memory ADDR. X2 is stored at ADDR and X1 is stored at ADDR+CELL.

9.4   String operators

code count   \ addr -- addr+1 len

Given the address of a counted string in memory this word will return the address
of the first character and the length in characters of the string.

CODE CMOVE \ source dest len -- ; copy memory areas

Copy U bytes of memory forwards from C-ADDR1 to C-ADDR2.

CODE CMOVE>   \ source dest len -- ; copy memory areas

As CMOVE but working in the opposite direction, copying the last character in the
string first.

: FILL   \ addr len char --

Fill LEN bytes of memory starting at ADDR with the byte information specified as
CHAR.

: (")   \ -- addr ; in-line string follows caller, and skip it

Return the address of a counted string that is inline after the CALLING word, and
adjust the CALLING word's return address to step over the inline string.

See the definition of (.") for an example.
The runtime action compiled by C".

: (C")   \ -- c-addr

The runtime action compiled by S".

: (S")   \ -- c-addr u

9.5   Umbilical versions of defining words

here is-action-of constant The runtime action for a CONSTANT.
here is-action-of variable The runtime action for a VARIABLE.
here is-action-of user
The runtime action of a USER variable.

: u#   \ "<uservar>" -- offset ; u# <uservar>

Return the offset of a USER variable in the user area.

here is-action-of value \ -- n ; default returns the value The runtime action
of a VALUE.

: CRASH   **\ -- ; used as default action of DEFERred word**

The default action of a DEFERed word. A NOOP.

here is-action-of DEFER \ Comp: "<spaces>name"

-- ; Run: i*x -- j*x The runtime action of a DEFERred word.

9.6 Interrupt handling

The interrupt handling words are just code generators in the cross compiler and have
no target versions.

10 MSP430 library

libraries	\ resolve required forward references
include %CpuDir%\lib430	\ include %CommonDir%\library
	\ for standalone apps
include %CommonDir%\uflib	\ for Umbilical apps
end-libs	

The library file LIB430.FTH can be used between LIBRARIES and END-LIBS to resolve outstanding forward references. See the Forth 6 manual for more details of the library mechanism.

code save-int   \ -- n ; save interrupt status
  Geturn interrupt status and then disable interrupts. Use [I and I] for new code.

code restore-int   \ n -- ; restore interrupt
  Restore state returned by SAVE-INT. Use [I and I] for new code.

: init-iow   \ addr --
  Copy the contents of the I/O set up table to an I/O device. The data is written as 16 bit words. See also INIT-IOB. Each element of the table is of the form addr (cell) followed by data (cell). The table is terminated by an address of 0. A table of a single 0 address performs no action.

: init-iob   \ addr --
  Copy the contents of the I/O set up table to an I/O device. The data is written as 8 bit bytes. See also INIT-IOW. Each element of the table is of the form addr (cell) followed by data (cell). The table is terminated by an address of 0. A table of a single 0 address performs no action.

11 USCI serial driver

The file *MSP430Lite\Drivers\serUSCIp.fth* contains the code for a polled serial driver.

11.1 Baud rate calculation

: genUSCIlf \ baud clock -- brx brsx
Generate the baud rate values for low frequency baud rate settings.
The word can only be executed while interpreting in the cross compiler.

: genUSCIos \ baud clock -- brx brfx
Generate the baud rate values for oversampling baud rate settings.
The word can only be executed while interpreting in the cross compiler.

11.2 UART0

: key?0 \ -- flag
Return true if UART0 received a character.

: key0 \ -- char
Wait for character from UART0 and return it.

: emit0 \ char --
Send a character through UART0.

: type0 \ c-addr len --
Send a string through UART0.

: cr0 \ --
Perform CR on UART0.

console0-speed system-speed genUSCIlf equ BRS0 equ BRX0
Generate the baud rate values for UART0.

: init-ser \ --
Configure UART0. This word can be hardware dependent.
The version here assumes USCI A0 on P1.1 and P1.2.

create Console0 \ -- addr ; OUT managed by upper driver
The device vector for UART0.

Console0 constant Console
Defines UART0 as the default system console.

11.3 UART1

: key?1   \ -- flag
Return true if UART1 received a character.

: key1   \ -- char
Wait for character from UART1 and return it.

: emit1   \ char --
Send a character through UART1.

: type1   \ c-addr len --
Send a string through UART1.

: cr1   \ --
Perform CR on UART1.

console1-speed system-speed genUSCIIf equ BRS1 equ BRX1
Generate the baud rate values for UART1.

: init-ser1   \ --
Configure UART1. This word can be hardware dependent. The version here assumes USCI A1. No port selection is made. This code is only compiled if another version has not been defined.

create Console1   \ -- addr ; OUT managed by upper driver
The device vector for UART1.

Console1 constant Console
Defines UART1 as the default system console.

11.3   Initialisation

: init-ser   \ --
Initialise the serial channels.

12 Ticker using watchdog timer

The ticker interrupt is provided in *LedTickLP2553.fth*.

: ticks   (-- n) <ticks> @ ;
    Return current clock value in milliseconds. This can be treated as
    a 16 bit unsigned value that will wrap when it overflows.

equ TickHz   \ -- hz
    Ticker speed in Hertz

1000 TickHz / equ Tick-Ms   \ -- ms
    Milliseconds per tick.

variable LedActive   \ -- addr
    Set true for LEDs to flash on the timer. Set this to false (zero) when you want to
    use the LEDs yourself.

Proc WDT-isr
Assembler coded interrupt service routine.

add .w	**# Tick-ms & <ticks>**	
add .w	**# Tick-ms &**	
	LedTimer	
cmp eq, if,	**# #1000 & LedTimer**	\ 1 second timeout
mov .w	**# 0 & LedTimer**	\ reset timer
cmp ne, if,	**# 0 & LedActive**	\ if enabled
xor .b	**# $41 & P1OUT**	\ toggle LEDs
endif, endif, reti		
end-code		

WDT-isr WDT_vec !

: Start-Clock   \ --
    Start the ticker interrupt.

: Stop-Clock   \ --
    Stop the ticker interrupt

: green-on   \ -- ; **P1.6**
     Turn green LED on.

: green-off   \ -- ; **P1.6**
     Turn green LED off.

: red-on   \ -- ; **P1.0**
     Turn red LED on.

: red-off   \ -- ; **P1.0**
     Turn red LED off.

13   Device drivers

This chapter documents a number of simple device drivers that can be added to the system, either by cross-compilation or by direct compilation onto the target.

13.1 Basic port usage

See the file *Drivers\gpio2553.fth*.

The user words are as follows:

- HI and LO configure the port bit for output.
- BIT? does not configure the port bit for input.
- SETIN configures the port bit for input.
-

P1IN CONSTANT PORT1   \ -- addr
    Base of Port 1.

P2IN CONSTANT PORT2   \ -- addr
    Base of Port 2

: HI   \ bit port --
    Set bit high.

: LO   \ bit port --

: SETIN   \ bit port --
    Set pin to input. Deselect other functions.

: BIT?   \ bit port --- f
    Return the state of the bit in the port.

13.2 Port counting using interrupts

See the file *Drivers\gpio2553.fth*.
The notation is: bit port startcount
The code assumes that interrupts are enabled elsewhere.

VARIABLE P1COUNT   \ -- addr
    Holds the count for Port 1.

VARIABLE P2COUNT   \ -- addr
    Holds the count for Port 2.

: STARTCOUNT   (bit port --)
    Start counting transitions for the given bit and port.
: STOPCOUNT   (port --)
    Stop counting transitions on the given port.

13.3 Simple ADC driver

See the file *Drivers\adc2553.fth*. The driver is not clever. It does all the setting up for each conversion - there is no separate set up word. It Leaves I/O pins in analogue mode until the next conversion. Be careful not to do a conversion on a digital pin. The supply voltage is used as the reference. 0 corresponds to 0V, 1023 corresponds to VCC.

: ATOD   \ channel# -- value
    DO a conversion on the given ADC channel (0..7) and return the value.

13.4 PWM

See the file *Drivers\pwm2553.fth*. The code sets up for three possible channels of 10 bit PWM for 20 pin device. The PWM frequency is about 7.5KHz.
Use P1.6PWM, P2.1PWM or P2.4PWM to initialise the relevant port and timer. P1.6 uses Timer0, the other two pins use Timer1. It is best to use P2.1 and P2.4 first to keep the other timer free. Once initialised, use P1.6DUTY, P2.1DUTY or P2.4DUTY to set the duty cycle.

: P1.6DUTY   \ value --
    Set the duty cycle on P1.6, $0..3FF.

: P1.6PWM   \ duty --
    Start PWM on pin 1.6, where *duty* is $0..3FF

: P2.1PWM   \ duty --
    Start PWM on pin 2.1, where *duty* is $0..3FF

: P2.4PWM   \ duty --
    Start PWM on pin 2.4, where *duty* is $0..3FF

Index

(page numbers left as in original MPE PDF)

init-iob	41
init-iow	41
init-ser	43, 44
init-ser1	44
interpret	29
invert	13
is	29
is-action-of	27, 40

j	10, 37

key	20
key?	20
key?0	43
key?1	43
key0	43
key1	43

last	20
later	31
leave	10
ledactive	45
literal	28
lo	47
loop	27
lshift	13

m*	12, 38
m/	38
max	37
min	37
mod	12, 38
move	27
ms	31

within?	37
word	27
words	27

xdp	20
xor	12

10 – One Alternative Forth is 4e4th

VFX is a commercial Forth package
There are MANY different Forth Compiler versions.

Native – running on the processor where the application is executed
Cross Compiler – developing on a PC for example, code THEN running on an Embedded Board
Umbilical Connection – just a minimum of code on the target.

As there are many free non-commercial versions available, there had to be a choice to cover this aspect of Forth.
The choice was easy – 4e4th, designed for Education.
Dirk and Michael helped me quite a bit, and as well Dirk's 4e4th IDE does not have to be installed but the exe runs as well ofF a USB stick.
Dirk sent me a TI Launchpad for the TI MSP430G2553 to start.
Reason for this choice? Very easy to start with and as well to do an own PCB board. MSP430G2553 is one of the few Microcontroller chips that are available in a small Dual-in-Line package.
My Forth Journey started from there at the time.
This lead to an activity with the IET, to design a processor board that can be solderd together by scouts and guides. This design resulted in the **MicroBox**. A small battery driven controller board that can be soldered together easily. And a cheap enclosure had to be found that fits – a TicTac Box. For more details about the MicroBox see the 4e4th manual 11b. There is a circuit diagram and the PCB layout.
3 extra links to the activity with the IET at Scouts Jamboree 2015 in the UK:
You find it on the Forth-ev.de website
https://wiki.forth-ev.de/doku.php/en:projects:microbox:start
Or the IET video direct link   https://tv.theiet.org/?videoid=7386
At Eurocircuits.com – they supplied 300 boards foc for the event.
http://www.eurocircuits.com/blog/eurocircuits-supports-iet-activity-at-peakcamp-201/
EuroTech supported this project with 1000 PCBs – free of charge.

11a – 4e4th Manual 1

Forth for Education
– 4E4th and 4E4th IDE

Dirk Bruehl   Dirk@4E4th.eu   http://www.4E4th.com

First Steps with 4E4th

**Installing 4E4th on the MSP430-LaunchPad
and on MicroBox using LP or the 6 wires.
Documentation slightly adapted for MicroBox**

Here our twelve step program to get 4E4th onto a brand-new MSP430-LaunchPad with an MSP430G2553 chip:
Requirements:
A LaunchPad with **MSP430G2553** Microprocessor and **4E4th-IDE** on Windows XP.

Here it starts:
1. Start Windows XP PC and 4E4th-IDE for Windows XP..
2. Click on 4E4th-IDE Menu
    LaunchPad / Preparing LaunchPad Connection.
3. Unpack MSP430-LaunchPad: cut foil, take out circuit board
    and take out USB-Cable hidden under cardboard cover.
4. Check HW | UART position of RX/TX-Jumper,
    turn by 90° if necessary.
5. Connect USB-Cable out of MSP430-LaunchPad box
    to MSP430-LaunchPad PCB.
6. Connect USB-Cable to PC - green Power-LED lights,
    red and green LEDs flash.
7. MSP430 Application UART Hardware Wizard appears on screen:
    If not already set, click on *"Install Software automatically"*,
    Click on button *"Next>"* - it will need some time until Software is
    found.
8. A message will come up telling the MSP430 Application UART
    has not passed Windows Logo testing to verify its compatibility
    with Windows XP.
    Click on button *"Continue Anyway"*.

Installation will need some seconds.

Click on button *"Finish"*.

9. Some messages are coming, telling that hardware is ready for use. Proceed with 4E4th-IDE.

10. Click on 4E4th-IDE Menu
LaunchPad / FLASH the LaunchPad / 4e4th.a43

11. Popup ** *All your Forth Words will be lost* **
Proceed with FLASHING the 4e4th?
Click on button *"Yes"*.

12. Flashing needs several seconds, when ready,
message *"Flashing 4e4th done -*
checking connections now" shows up.
If everything is okay, the message
"4e4thFLASH connections checked !
Click 'Start' button to connect to target !"
shows up.

Now 4E4th is installed on the LaunchPad!

The red and the green LED are lit as long as the LaunchPad
is connected to the PC and no program HAS switched off an LED.

For better explanation the same points again, but now with additional pictures:

1. Start the 4E4th-IDE:,

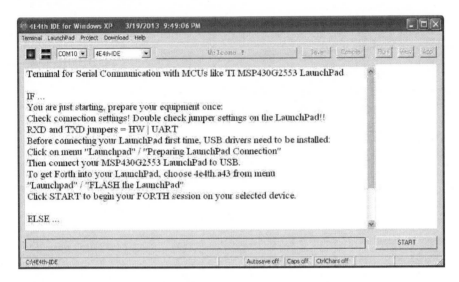

2. Click on Menu LaunchPad / Preparing LaunchPad Connection.

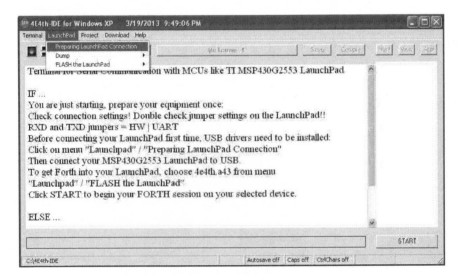

A batch-program does this fully automatic:

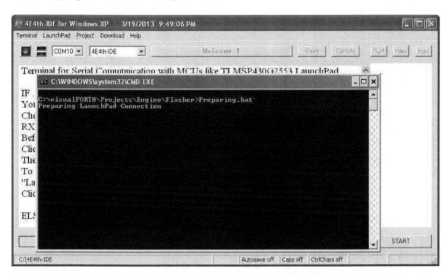

When the batch-program has finished, this message comes up:

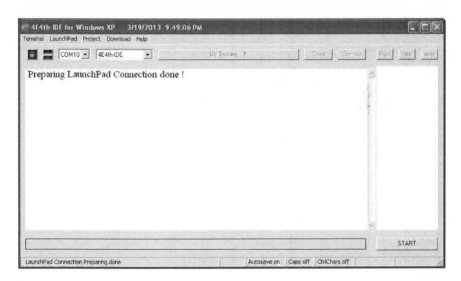

3. Unpack MSP430-LaunchPad: cut foil, take out circuit board and take out USB-Cable hidden under cardboard cover.
4. Check all of the jumpers: the HW UART position of the RX/TX-Jumpers might have to be changed, turned by 90° if necessary.

On delivery you will see that all jumpers from VCC- and TEST-Jumpers to RXD and TXD are all vertically placed on the LaunchPad.

Please change the RXD- and TXD-Jumpers;

these 2 on the left have to be horizontal.

Here see the right jumper setting for the HW UART used by 4e4th:

In this picture on bottom left you see the USB connector:

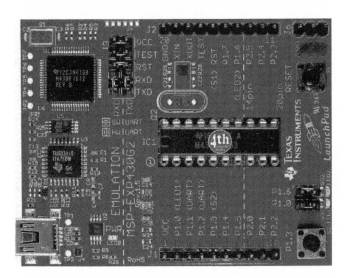

There the USB-Cable has to be connected first.

5. Connect the USB-Cable out of the LaunchPad box to the MSP430-LaunchPad.

6. Connect USB-Cable to the PC - green Power-LED lights, red and green LEDs flash.

7. MSP430 Application UART Hardware Wizard appears on screen:
   If not already set, click on "Install Software automatically",
   Click on button "Next>"
   - it will need some time till Software is found.

8. A message will probably come up telling that
the MSP430 Application UART has not passed Windows Logo
testing to verify its compatibility with Windows XP.
Click on button "*Continue Anyway*". The Installation will need
some seconds.
"Found New Hardware Wizard" finally shows
"Completing the Found New Hardware Wizard"
- click on button "*Finish*".

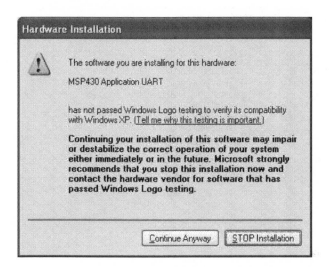

9. Some messages are coming, telling that hardware is ready for use. Proceed with 4E4th-IDE.

10. Click on Menu *LaunchPad / FLASH the LaunchPad / 4e4th.a43*

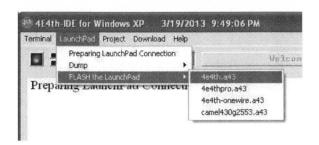

11. Popup ** *All your Forth Words will be lost*
    ** *Proceed with FLASHING the 4e4th?*

Click on button "*Yes*":

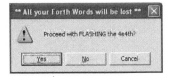

12. Flashing of the chip needs several seconds:

When ready, the message

"*Flashing 4e4th done - checking connections now*" shows.

If everything is okay, this message follows:

"*4e4thFLASH connections checked*

- click 'Start' button to connect to target !"

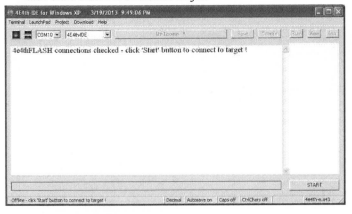

Now 4E4th software is installed on the LaunchPad!

The red and the green LED are lit as long as the LaunchPad is connected to the PC and no program switched off an LED.

When these 12 installation points have been successful, 4E4th and the 4E4th-IDE are ready to use.

A click on "START", and the 4E4th LaunchPad is connected:

Both LEDS on the IDE change to green.

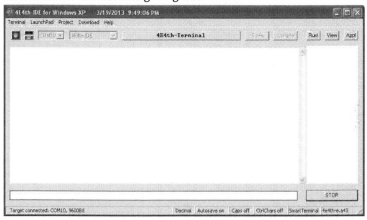

The cursor is blinking at the entry line.

Everytime when actuating the PC Enter key, 4E4th reports with "ok" and a new line:

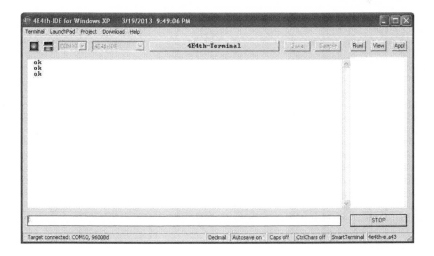

Now our adventure "Programming" is ready to start!

Our first example is from Leo Brodie's book "Starting Forth":

: Star 42 emit ;

Type it into the IDE entry line at the bottom and hit the Enter key.

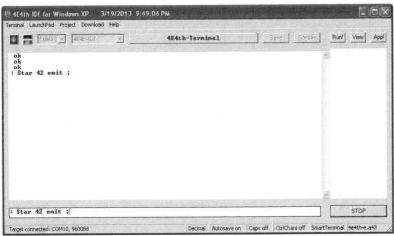

Explanation:

The colon marks the start of a new Word-Definition.

"Star" is this new Word, the name of this new Word.

All 4E4th texts are coded in ASCII-CODE, 42 is the ASCII-Code for the Star: *

"*emit*" means send to the terminal.

The semicolon marks the end of this new Word-Definition.

This is really easy to comprehend:

With this line "**: Star 42 emit ;**"

we define a new word, which sends a Star * to our Terminal – it's so simple!

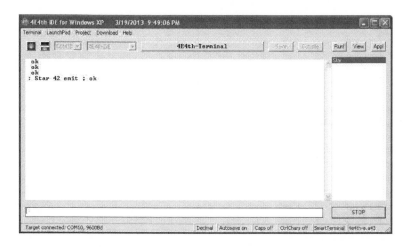

We type this line into the 4E4th-IDE entry line and actuate the PC Enter key:

4E4th answers with ok, the entry line is empty again, and in the white field, on the right side, the Word "Star" is shown in white on blue. In this box the new Words defined are shown.

A click on "*Run!*" bottom on the right, and the Word Star appears in the next Terminal line, followed by "* ok" in the second next Terminal line:

Now we have written and tested our first "Program"! Cool!

This first program is named *"Star"*, the Word, which gave its name to this Program. Therefore from now on we call it "Word" instead of Program.

Another kind of testing:

We type the Word "Star" into our entry line

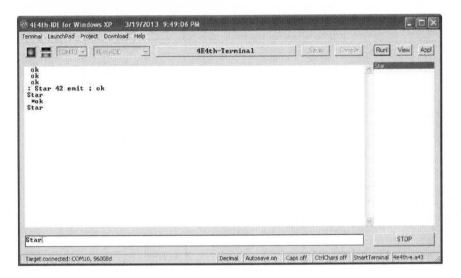

and actuate the PC Enter key:

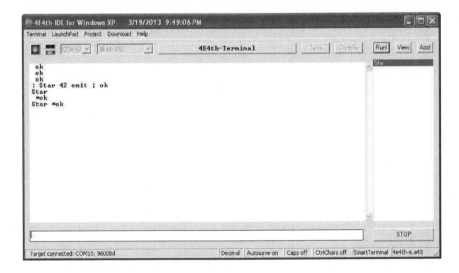

This time we see the Word and the Star in one line, followed by "*ok".
Now we are sure that Programming works and we are able to proceed:

: Stars 0 do Star loop ;

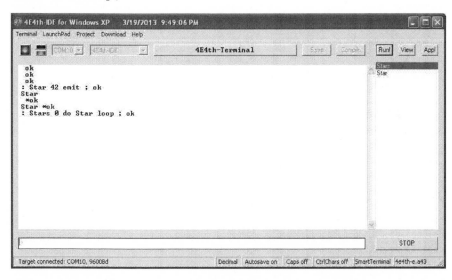

Hint: We can use Copy/Paste to copy this line into our entry line!

The whole line will now be sent to our microprocessor.

We now have a new Word "*Stars*" on top of our Word List, and here how it works:
This Program starts with zero, that's what the "*o*" is telling.
Then it does (*do*) something: sending a "*Star*", and this function will be repeated in a "*loop*".
4E4th has to be informed how often to repeat, that means it needs the number of Stars to send, before the Word "*Stars*" will be started.
To accomplish this, type a number into our entry line, let's say 12:

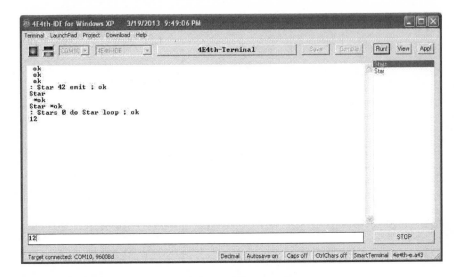

As usual we actuate the PC Enter key – 4E4th answers with "ok":

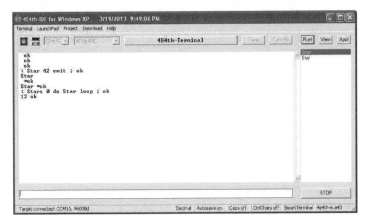

With a click on "*Run!*" the Word "*Stars*" will be transferred to the Microprocessor, shown in the Terminal window, and the Microprocessor answers with 12 Stars, followed by "ok":

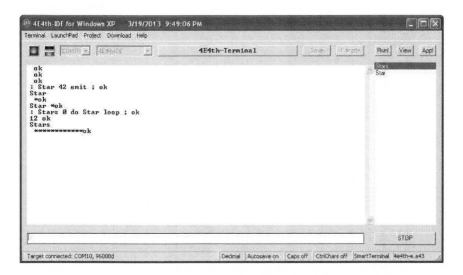

By the way, when we like to know, if 4E4th took our number, then we can ask by typing ".s":

So, type a number, actuate the PC Enter key, type ".s", and actuate the PC Enter key again:

4E4th answers after ".s" with

<1> 123 ok

<1> means, that 4E4th got *one* number. This number was 123.

Then we type in "Stars":

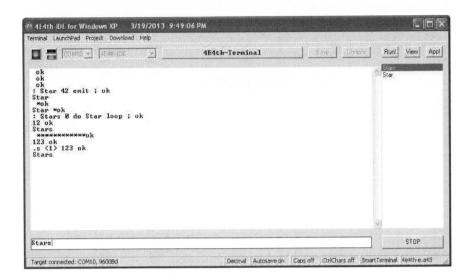

Actuating the PC Enter key, 4E4th answers, following the Word "Stars" with 123 Stars and "ok":

Stars

****
**ok

These first examples clearly show, that the PC Enter key has to be actuated to tell 4E4th to evaluate what we typed into our entry line.

Each character, which we typed into the 4E4th-IDE entry line, will be sent to our 4E4th LaunchPad Microprocessor immediately, and 4E4th echoes each character back to our IDE – printable characters from 4E4th will then be shown in our Terminal window.

With actuating the PC Enter key, the input of a line is closed, and 4E4th will react on what is written in this line. Later we will report how that works.

I am sure now that I don't have to mention the PC Enter key any more.

To actuate the PC Enter key at the end of a line should be natural now, of course.

Let's go forward with our Program – here are the next lines:

: Margin CR 5 Spaces ;

: Beam Margin 5 Stars ;

: Blip Margin Star ;

: F Beam Blip Beam Blip Blip Blip ;

Of course it makes sense to test each Word after each Word-Definition.

These Words don't expect a number.

Click on "*Run!*" after each line to look what this Word does.

This is really simple and fast, using Copy/Paste for each line, followed by actuating the Enter key and test with a simple click on "*Run!*":

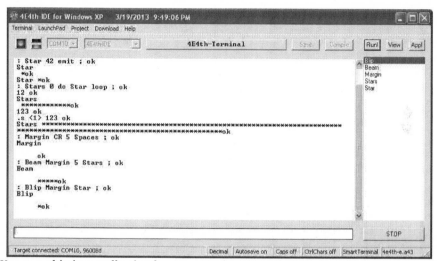

You see, this is a really simple programming example, to learn the first steps with 4E4th. The last line paints an F, using stars:

136

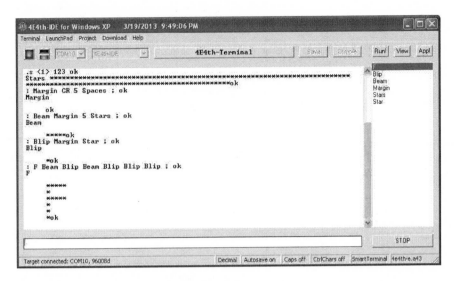

It bothers me that the "ok" is touching the last star.
To make the "F" look better, we should change it!

Nothing simpler than that:

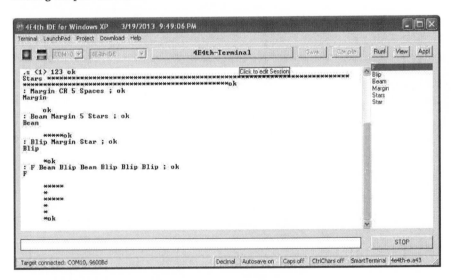

A click on the wide "4E4th-Terminal" bar above the Terminal window switches to the
Editor Mode:

LEDs have changed to red, as this is a local activity.

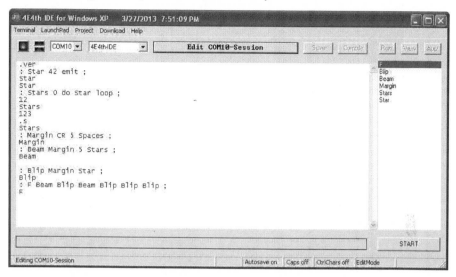

Now the caption of this bar has changed to "*Edit COMxx-Session*", and our text, which we typed is shown in the Terminal window, written in another font, and we are able to do changes.

That's what we do now. The second line from bottom is:

: F Beam Blip Beam Blip Blip Blip ;

We simply put a "cr and a space" before the semicolon:

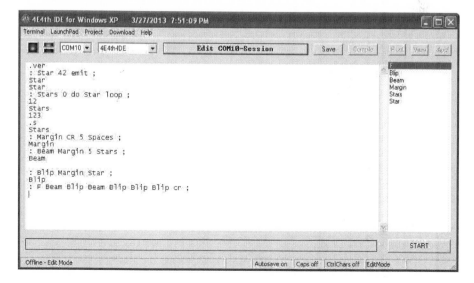

"cr" is a shortcut for "Carriage Return", inherited from the old times of teletypes. With the "cr" inserted, this line looks like on the picture above.

To be on the safe side, we have removed the single character "F" in the last line.

Now a clue to be remembered: between two Words always has to be a space – Colon and Semicolon are counted as Words, too.

This is the only way to allow 4E4th to be able to read each Word and recognize it.

Next we click on button "*Save*" (right of the "*Editor*" bar), and then button "*Compile*" two times

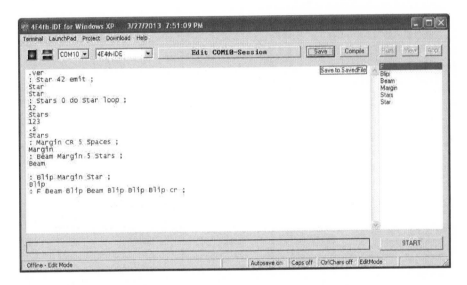

The first click on "*Compile*" switches 4E4th-IDE back to Terminal-Modus:

The LEDs change back to green

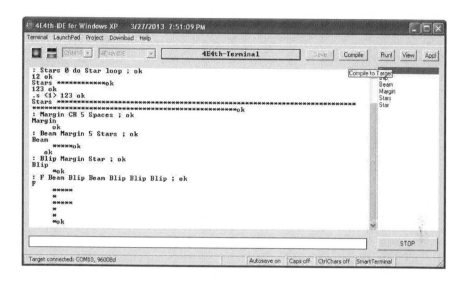

The second click is followed by a Popup asking
"Wipe before Download?":

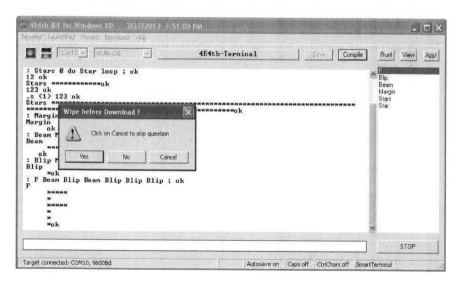

We don't like to compile everything again, so we click on the middle button *"No"*.

Doing this, only the line which we changed will be sent to 4E4th:

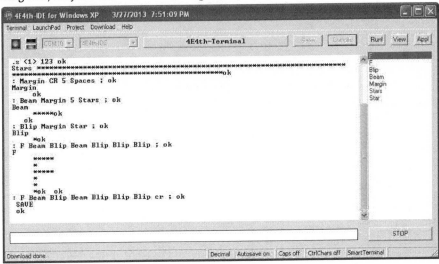

A click on "*Run!*" shows, our operation was successful:

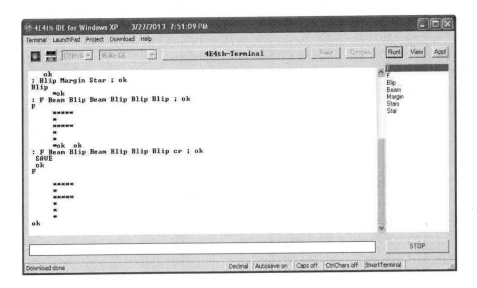

Now a final Test!

A click on *Terminal* (top left), and the *Terminal-Menu* shows up:

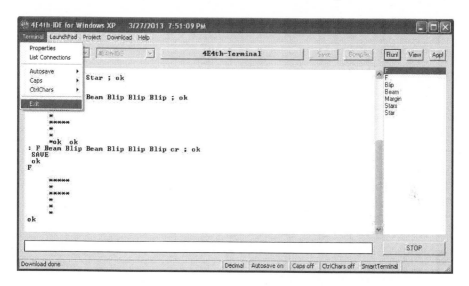

A click on *Exit* ends our 4E4th-IDE-Session ("session" is the name for sitting at our computer for a while).

Then we pull the USB-plug of the Launchpad-cable from our PC, and the LaunchPad LEDs are off. Of course, without power nothing works.
To see what happens, we connect our 4E4th-LaunchPad, which we used for our first programming steps with our PC again;

after waiting for ten seconds or more to give our PC the chance to check that our USB connection was interrupted first and then connected again - all three LEDs on the board are lit again now.

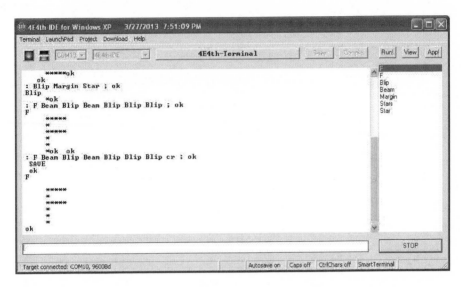

Then we start our *4E4th-IDE.exe* – a click on the button *"START"* bottom right, and our work appears in our Terminal window again (see picture above).
A click on *"Run!"* shows that our work wasn't been in vain.
It still works!

Now our Programming Adventure is really starting to go!

To have some fun, we prepared a Morse program.
We connect a little 8Ohm speaker to MSP430-LaunchPad pins P1.4 and P1.5, and there we go:
This time we choose a ready-made Program, and we send it with *"Download"* from the PC to our 4E4th-LaunchPad.

With a click on menu *"Download / Selected File"* the well-known Windows-File-Selection appears:

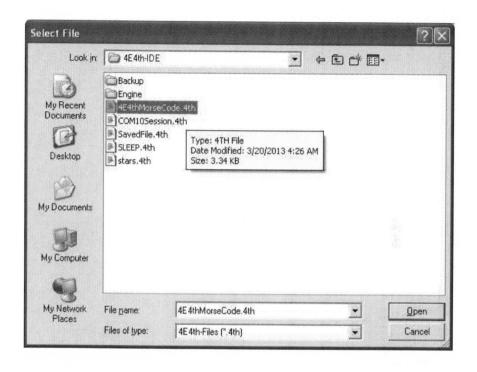

A click on 4E4thMorseCode.4th
and then on "*Open*",
and the Download starts:

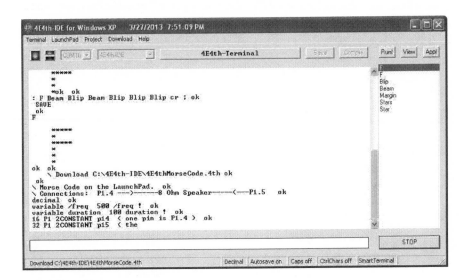

The Download needs some time – it needs a bit of patience.

The Download has to be ready for testing – soon it is done:

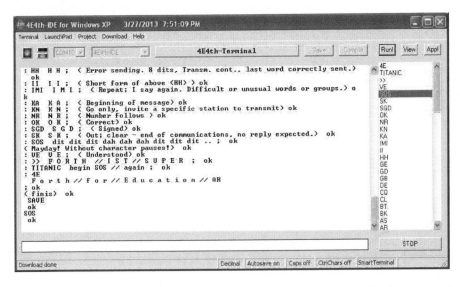

A click on "SOS" and "*Run!*", and we hear an SOS – as long as the speaker is connected in the right manner – and the red LED is blinking SOS.

We can type in single characters into the Terminal entry line and hear the sound pattern. It works with single digits too, but these need an underscore to be recognized. Of course we can click on characters, digits, and combinations to make them sound as Morse code.

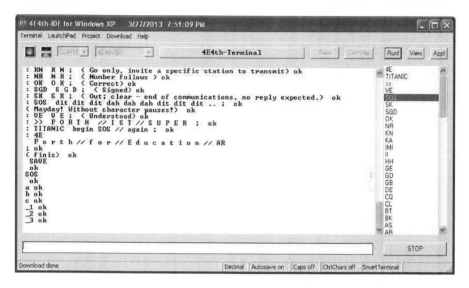

For completion we click on "OK" at the Wordlist (right panel), then a click on "*App!*", and from now on we will be greeted with an "OK" Morsecode each time when we hit the LaunchPad RESET button or when we connect our LaunchPad to power again:

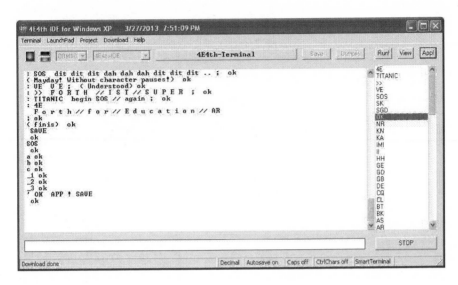

Now we have a complete Program which starts by itself!

Congratulations! You have done it – even if it needed some patience!

Salisbury, 11/24/2012 - updated 3/27/2013   Dirk Bruehl.

Exeter,UK 19 March 2016 – changed to A5 size and MicroBox added by Juergen Pintaske

Preliminary Version – change without Notice

11b - 4e4th Manual 2

4E4th and 4E4th IDE
Forth for Education

Dirk Bruehl   Dirk@4E4th.eu   http://www.4E4th.com

4E4th-IDE Instructions

This manual is slightly modified from the original to ensure than the MicroBox requirements are covered. The MicroBox project was actually triggered by Dirk's IDE and 4e4th – Juergen Pintaske 2016

MicroBox consists of a small PCB with 2 AAA batteries in a TicTac box, just the minimum parts of the TI Launchpad, connected to the PC via an FTDI USB-to-TTL cable and can be battery operated.

For now the transfer of the Forth program image has to be done via one of two options:
To flash the TI MSP2553 chip in the Launchpad

and then move the chip to the MicroBox,

  or

connect the 6 MicroBox connections

   Ground - +3.3V – Rx – Tx – Test – Reset

via a cable to the Launchpad for programming the Forth Kernel into the Chip in the MicroBox. This then replaces the TI Launchpad.

Schematic MicroBox   PCB Bottom View   PCB Top View

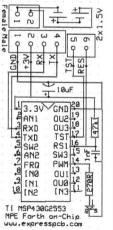 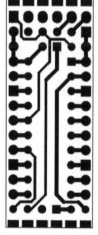 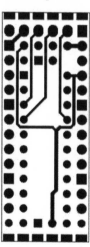 

Here a first look at the 4E4th-IDE:

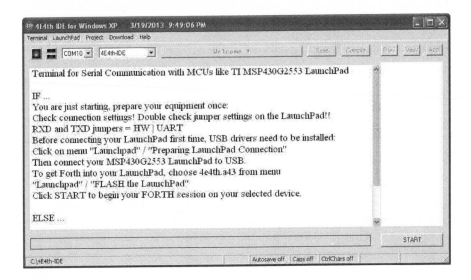

This is what the 4E4th-IDE looks like when 4E4th-IDE.exe has been started for the first time, and a LaunchPad is connected to the computer.

The red LED shows that the 4E4th-IDE is not ready to communicate with the "target", which is the 4E4th-LaunchPad.

For a quick START to get connected with the target, click on the START button

The LEDs switch to green and you can start programming.

To give you the best programming experience, I will write about all of the 4E4th-IDE controls, which will help you to have a great programming experience.

There are: menus, buttons, selections, the Terminal screen, the Input line, and the Wordlist.

But before starting a description, a brief overview to show how you can work with the 4E4th-IDE. A brief description about using the 4E4th-IDE was already given in "First Steps with 4E4th". Here are now some new exiting possibilities:
We can use the Terminalinput Box to type in our programs:

Or we can use several Download functions which will be described later.

Let's assume that we downloaded our Stars.4th file, and our screen looks like this:

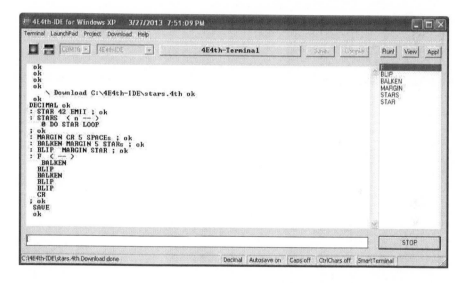

The second last line is **"SAVE"** – the saving will be done each time automatically after a file download is finished. This feature may be switched off.
The status line in the picture above shows "Autosave on", so this feature is active.
The last defined word was "F", and this word is marked blue in the Wordlist on the right side of the 4E4th-IDE.

There are three little buttons on top of this Wordlist:

Run! – Run the Word selected

View – Show the parts of the Word selected

App! – Run this Word immediately
        when the Launchpad is reset or switched on

Let's first click on the first one, **"Run!"** - a click on "Run!" starts the program belonging to the marked Word, showing the letter "F" painted by Stars:

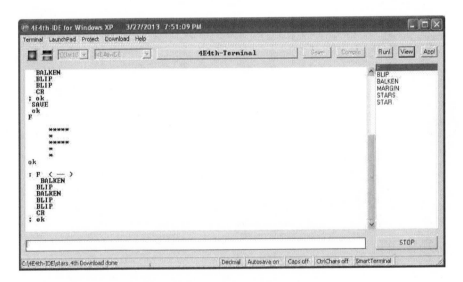

The next exercise is to click on the button "View":

The definition of "F" will be printed on the 4E4th–IDE screen again.

And last, but not least the third button, the most important one: "App!"

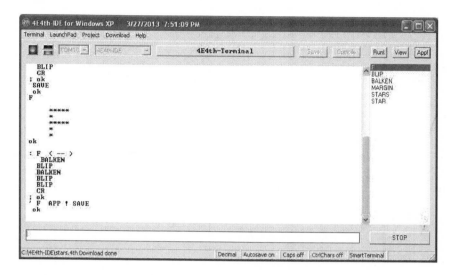

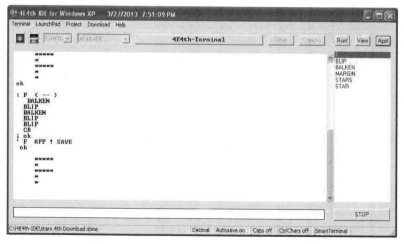

Normally we use this button **App!** only when our program is finished, to save it and to tell the 4E4th, that this Word marked in blue has to be started with each reset or power on.

To test this function now, we push the RESET button on the LaunchPad, and there it is:

Programming with Copy / Paste

Before we start programming with Copy / Paste, we make sure that we have a "clean" Forth core, and remove all previous programs that might have been included by using the word "wipe":

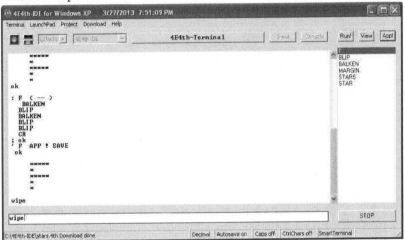

After a few seconds the 4e4th-IDE looks like this:

Now we copy a part of our file stars.4th

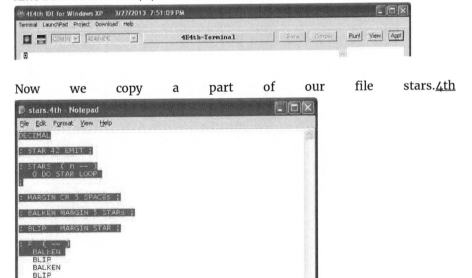

Run!

and click on Menu "Download – Clipboard – Until ;";
this sends all lines until the end of the first colon-definition to our target.
As we can see, that the button "Run!" is enabled, encouraging us to
   click on **Run!**

Next   - and the button "Next" is enabled.

A click on **"Run!"** starts the word, which is marked in the Wordlist, as usual:

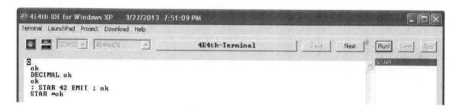

And several clicks on "Next" and "Run!" send the remaining copied code to our target
and test it, until the "Next" vanished – and this button is now named "Compile" and
disabled.
This shows that our Clipboard Download is exhausted.

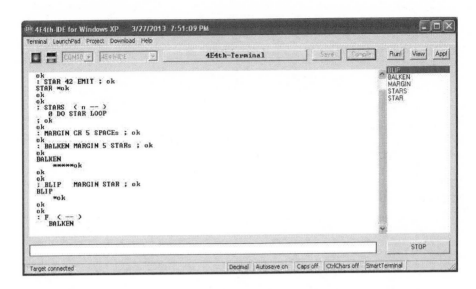

As we can see, "F" is only partly defined, because our copy didn't take the full file.

I am sure you have been wondering why I did this.
There was a reason for this: I like to show another method to finish this definition.
It is really easy: I click on "Run!" again! And as a result, the Word "BLIP" is added to F, then I mark the Word "BALKEN" and I click on "Run!" again. Here you see it:

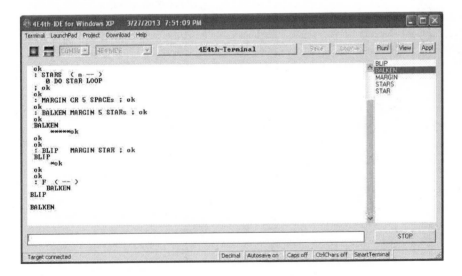

And when this definition is filled by adding "BLIP" three times, only a "cr ;" has to be typed via the Terminal input:

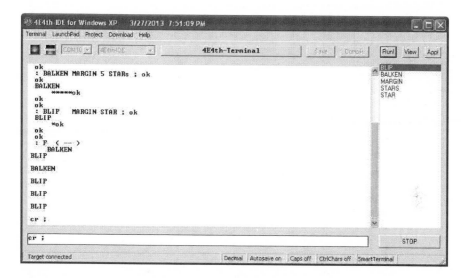

Activating the Enter key finally finishes the definition –

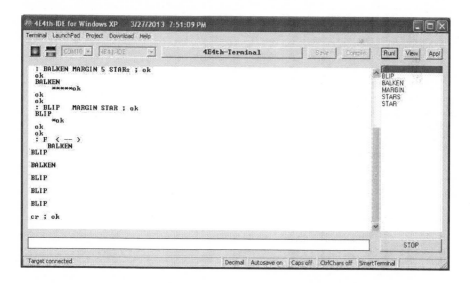

- and with another click on "Run!" the newly defined Word "F" will be started.

These pages show that programming with our 4E4th-IDE is much more convenient than by using a standard Terminal Emulator.

Terminal LaunchPad Project Download Help

Now back to our description of the 4E4th-IDE menu:

Menus:

Terminal LaunchPad Project Download Help

There are five different menus:
Terminal, LaunchPad, Project, Download, and Help.

The Terminal-Menu

Terminal has six sub menus:

"Properties",
"List Connections",
"Autosave",
"Caps",
"CtrlChars" – these have settable options,
the settings of these options will not be
saved
"Exit"

Terminal

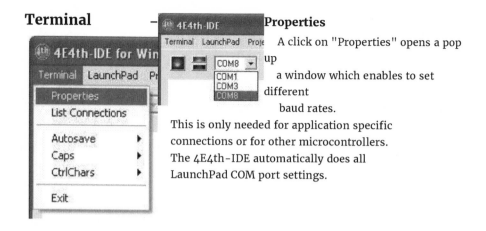

Properties

A click on "Properties" opens a pop up a window which enables to set different baud rates.

This is only needed for application specific connections or for other microcontrollers. The 4E4th-IDE automatically does all LaunchPad COM port settings.

The window "Terminal Properties" is added preparing for future extensions.

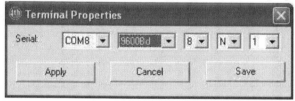

Terminal - List Connections

"List Connections" checks which COM ports are available, sets these COM ports to the COM port-display and selects the highest COM port, because in most cases this is the one connected to the LaunchPad.

In case the LaunchPad has a COM port with another number, this can be selected from the COM port display:

When starting 4E4th-IDE.exe, the connection check is automatically done.

In case the target has been connected
later, a click on   "List Connections" adds the
new COM port to be able to get connected.

Terminal - Autosave

When a file download is done, all Words
are automatically saved,
when closing a session, a pop up will ask
for saving, if not saved.
To switch this functionality off, click on
"Autosave off".

And remember: This setting on / off will
not be saved.

Terminal - Caps

To make the target correspondence
look the "old fashioned way",
or if Caps are needed,
click on "Caps on".

This setting will not be saved.

Terminal - CtrlChars

The "CtrlChars" setting allows
to see control characters sent to and from the
target.

There are four settings:

off

hex,

decimal, and

ASCII.

This setting will not be saved.

Terminal - Exit

A click on "Exit" will end the 4E4th-IDE session.
All entered data will be saved,
starting 4E4th-IDE.exe anew
will show the same data on screen again after a
click on "START".
No data will be lost, but the "Autosave", "Caps",
and "CtrlChars" settings will be
in the default state again.

The LaunchPad-Menu

LaunchPad has three
submenus:

"Preparing LaunchPad
Connection",

"Dump", and

"FLASH the LaunchPad".

LaunchPad - Preparing LaunchPad Connection

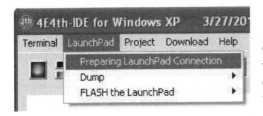 Preparing LaunchPad
Connection is needed,
when a LaunchPad is
connected to a PC for
the first time,

See the file "First Steps with 4E4th".
A link is found in the Help Menu.

LaunchPad - Dump

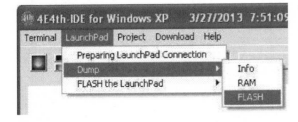 The "Dump" menu
allows to dump
memory areas of
the 4E4th micro.
There are three
different areas
which may be dumped:

Info,
RAM, and
FLASH.
The latter shows how Forth Words are arranged.
To get connected to the target after a Dump again, click on "START", eventually on
"STOP" first.

LaunchPad - FLASH the LaunchPad

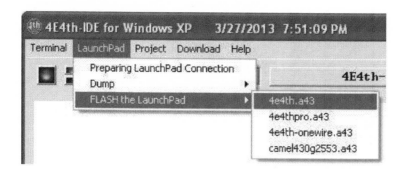

This menu point is used to " FLASH the LaunchPad"
and allows to put 4E4th Forth program onto the LaunchPad,
  using one of these files, which are
  residing in the folder \Engine\Flasher.

More information about this is provided in menu
"Help" – "First Steps with 4E4th"

The Project-Menu

Project has six submenus:

"Show selected File",
"Show Saved File",
"Clear Screen",
"Clear List of Words",
"Save Screen as File", and
"Start new Project".

Project - Show selected File

A click on
"Show selected File",
opens a Windows pop up
to allow editing the content
of a selected 4th file
on the 4E4th-IDE screen.

Project - Show Saved File

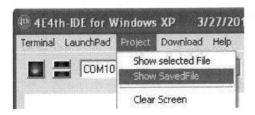

A click on
"Show Saved File" allows
to edit the contents of the
file SavedFile.
4th on the 4E4th- IDE
screen, which
has been saved with Edit.

Project - Clear Screen

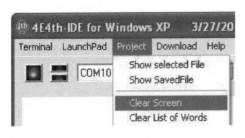

A click on "Clear Screen"
clears the
Terminal screen
and temporarily the
Edit screen.

Project - Clear List of Words

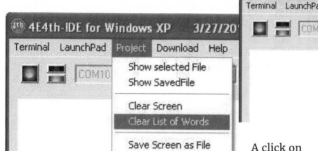

A click on
"Clear List of Words"
clears the Word List
(right panel).

Project - Save Screen as File

"Save Screen as File"
opens a Windows pop up
to allow saving the current
content of the 4E4th-IDE
screen.

File endings will be
attached automatically.

Project - Start new Project

"Start new Project" opens a
Windows pop up
to allow to start a new
project:

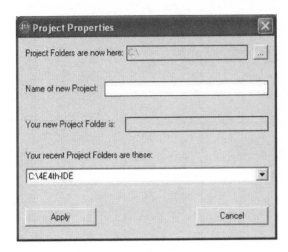

To start a new project, simply type the name of your new project – in this example this name is "MyProject" - into the input field right to "Name of new Project:"

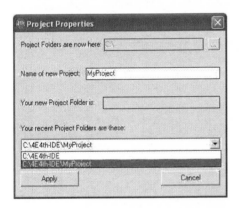

A click on "Apply" establishes this new folder and shows it at the Project Window.

The Download-Menu

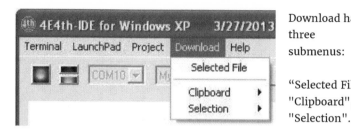

Download has three submenus:

"Selected File", "Clipboard", and "Selection".

Download - Selected File

A click on "Selected File" opens a Windows pop up to allow a file to be downloaded.
Only 4E4th-Files and folders will be shown:

Download - Clipboard

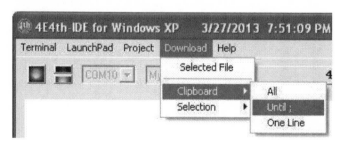

Download Clipboard has three submenus:

"All", "Until ;" and "One Line".

Download Clipboard allows to copy & paste words, programs, or a part of programs. Simply select and copy the words you like to transfer to the 4E4th target chip, and click on
"Download" "Clipboard" "All"
in case you like to download the whole text at once.
There are two other options for downloading data into the MSP430 chip:
A line by line download with a click on "One Line"
or a download for colon definition by colon definition
    with a click on "Until ;", repeating this until all text has been transferred.

Click on button "Next" to proceed.
A compile error will stop this download.

Download - Selection

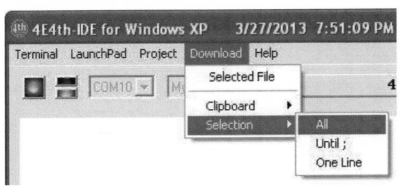

Download Selection has three submenus:
    "All",
    "Until ;" and
    "One Line".
Download Selection allows to paste words, programs, or parts of programs from the 4E4th-IDE screen. Simply mark these words which you like to transfer to the target chip on the 4E4th-IDE screen,
and click on "Download" "Selection" "All" in case you like to download the whole text at once.
There are two other options:
A line by line download with a click on "One Line"
or a download for one colon definition for each click on "Until ;", until all text is transferred.
Click on button "Next" to proceed. A compile error will stop this download.

The Help-Menu

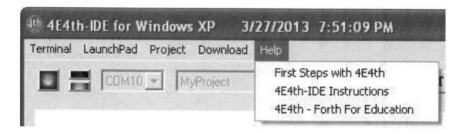

The "Help" menu has three submenus:
"First Steps with 4E4th",
"4E4th-IDE instructions" and
a web link to 4e4th.

Help Menu - First Steps with 4E4th

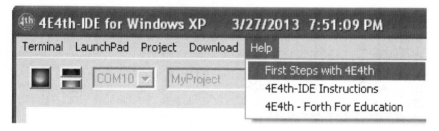

First Steps with 4E4th" loads 4E4th-IDE-StartNotes
  from the Internet.
  These 4E4th-IDE-StartNotes may be saved for later use.

  "4E4th-IDE instructions" loads the 4E4th-IDE-Instructions which
  you are just reading now, from the Internet.
  These 4E4th-IDE-Instructions may be saved for later use.

  "4E4th - Forth For Education" opens our 4e4th website for further
  information.

Salisbury, 1/7/2013 – updated 3/29/2013   Dirk Bruehl.
Reformatted and MicroBox added by Juergen Pintaske 2016-03-29
Preliminary Version – might change without Notice

11c – uMMT – Some small Example Code to try

Small examples help best. Here for the MSP430 board. Only a few Forth words are used to control the IO of the chip.

Set some IO bits. The Data Direction Register sets the data flow direction - here to ourput, and set this bit to HIGH and to LOW

The second part introduces the definition of Forth words to ease reading of the code.

This was intentionally written so it can be printed onto one page.

Not really necessary, but easy to copy and to print.

uMMT – The Main Code in short on One Page v7 2016_05_01

Easy for copy and paste - MPE VFX 430 LITE version, should work with 4e4th

\ Dictionary | C! | CSET | CCLR | @ | LSHIFT | DUP | DROP | MS |
\ | AND | OR | XOR |INVERT | RSHIFT | BEGIN | UNTIL | IF |
\ | : | ; | .S | . | U. | KEY? | ? | HEX | DECIMAL |
\ HEX \ change communication to HEX where needed – do not forget ! Error else
\ 11 22 33   \ put some data on to the stack
\ .S   \ and check it is there

\ 00 2E c! \ set port2 to just be GPIO, no internal specials used   \ setgpio
\ 80 2A cset \ set bit7 DDR to output.   40/20/10 for other bits   \ bit7out
\ 80 29 cset \ set bit 7 HIGH. Replace by 40/20/10 for other bits   \ bit7h
\ 80 29 cclr \ set bit 7 LOW. Replace by 40/20/10 for other bits   \ bit7l

\ variable OUTVA2   \ define a variable OUTV which holds some values
\ 77 OUTVA2 !   \ to test, load the variable with 77
\ Outva2 @ .   \ and display the data in OUTL – visible on output LEDs

\ : OUTL2 OUTVA2 @ 4 lshift 29 c! ; \ Output variable OUTV to OUTL \ to LEDs

\ 0F 2A cclr \ set upper nibble to OUT, lower nibble to IN   \ setoutin
\ 0F 2F cset \ enable the 4 internal resistors, inputs not open   \ enres
\ 0F 29 cset \ ensure the 4 INPUTS are enabled   \ set4in
: INIT2 00 2e c! F0 2a C! 0F 2F cset 0F 29 cset ; \ as one word \ init
: 4SHIFTL2 4 LSHIFT 0F OR ; reposition IN to OUT   \ 4shiftl
: INTOOUT INIT2 BEGIN 28 C@ 4SHIFTL2 29 C! KEY? UNTIL ;   \ intoout

\ 1000 ms 80 29 cset \ 1 second delay to set bit 7 high (set hex/decimal?)
\ 500 ms 80 29 cclr \ one half second delay after CR to set bit 7 to low

: DELAY begin dup ms 80 29 cset dup ms 80 29 cclr key? until drop; \x delay

DECIMAL \ set to decimal for easier calculations \   \ decimal
: DIT   80 29 cset 300 ms 80 29 cclr 100 ms ; \ LEDon 300ms,off 100 \ dit
: DAA   80 29 cset 900 ms 80 29 cclr 100 ms ; \ LEDon 900ms,off 100 \ daa
: SP   300 ms ; \ short pause between letters   \ sp
: LP   999 ms ; \ long pause between words   \ lp
: MorseSOS begin dit dit dit sp daa daa daa sp dit dit dit sp key? until ;
: AND01b BEGIN 28 c@ DUP 1 rshift AND 01 AND 4shiftl 29 c! key? until ;\and01
: OR01b BEGIN 28 C@ DUP 1 RSHIFT OR 01 AND 4SHIFTL 29 C! KEY? UNTIL ;   \ or01
: XOR01b BEGIN 28 C@ DUP 1 RSHIFT XOR 01 AND 4SHIFTL 29 C! KEY? UNTIL ; \xor01
: INVERT0b BEGIN 28 C@ INVERT 01 AND 4SHIFTL 29 C! KEY? UNTIL ; \ invo

: **ToSc** Decimal begin 1 . 1000 ms key? until ; \ to screen 1 1 / sec \ **tosc**

: **LedCount**

: **INITADC** 00 2E c! F0 2A c! 0F 2F cset 0F 29 cset ; \ Init our simple ADC
Variable ADCV   \ Define variable ADCV
: **ADC** initadc 0 ADCV ! BEGIN 1 ADCV +! 1 28 cget UNTIL ADCV @ . ; \ Go

Xxxx Variable ON   \ PWM OUT ON – values: DAC xxx1, SERVO xxx2, SOUND xxx3
Yyyy Variable OFF   \ PWM OUT OFF – values: DAC yyy1, SERVO yyy2, SOUND yyy3
: **DAC** begin ON @ 0 do loop 80 29 cset OFF @ 0 do loop 80 29 cclr key? until ;

: **FR** begin dup @ 0 do loop 80 29 cset dup @ 0 do loop 80 29 cclr key? until ;

: **TBD1**

: **TBD2**

Our Small Debugger

: **???** 2E @ . 2A @ . 28 @ . OUTV @ . 29 @ . base @ >r hex .S r> base ! ; \ ???
    \ GPIO DDR   INPUTS OUTV   LEDs   STACK

Other Words used: 0 commit – empty – freeled – flashled – application –

ExMark - Juergen Pintaske – www.exemark.com –

\ From here onwards starts a file INCLUDE which contains new words
\ First type WORDS, see which FORTH words are available, difference to later
\ generate folder *c:|ummt*, save this page to end with ForthED as file *INCLUDE*
\ in uMMT type *INCLUDE C:|ummt|inlcude*
\ this will read the file compile and include the new words
\   and add them to WORDS that were there before
\ now type WORDS again, the new WORDS added via INCLUDE are the first ones
\ new Words are: SETGPIO FREELED FLASHLED OUTV   OUTL   SETOUTIN INIT
\   BIT7OUT BIT7L BIT7H   BIT6OUT BIT6L BIT6H
\   BIT5OUT BIT5H BIT5L   BIT4OUT BIT4L BIT4H INTOOUT
\   4SHIFTL SET4IN SETOUTIN ENRES DELAY TOSC ???
\   DIT   DAA   SP   LP   MORSESOS

: freeled 0 ledactive ! ; \ decouple LED from Interrupt - free to be used
: flashled 1 ledactive ! ; \ back to interrupt driven LED

: setgpio 00 2e c! ;   \ set port2 to using the General Purpose IO only
\   - no internal specials used for now like counters ...
\ IO control for OUTPUT; we use in uMMT PORT2. 4 bits OUTPUT, 4 bits INPUT
\ uMMT using Port 1 needs 2a to xx and 29 to yy - NOT BIT 11 AND 12 AS RX TX
\ Bit7-out3 Bit6-out2 Bit5-out1 Bit4-out0 Bit3-in3 Bit2-in2 Bit1-in1 Bit0-in0
: bit7out 80 2a cset ; \ set bit 7 to be an output / Texas Instruments
: bit7h 80 29 cset ; \ set bit 7 to HIGH level / MSP430G2553 20 PIN DIL
: bit7l 80 29 cclr ; \ set bit 7 to LOW level / Plus 1 +   20 GND
: bit6out 40 2a cset ; \ set bit 6 to be an output / A0/x 2 10 26 19 O2
: bit6h 40 29 cset ; \ set bit 6 to HIGH level /   RX 3 11 27 18 O4
: bit6l 40 29 cclr ; \ set bit 6 to LOW level /   TX 4 12   17 Tst
: bit5out 20 2a cset ; \ set bit 5 to be an output /   S2 5 13   16 RESS1
: bit5h 20 29 cset ; \ set bit 5 to HIGH level /   AD4 6 14 17 15 S3
: bit5l 20 29 cclr ; \ set bit 5 to LOW level /   FRQ 7 15 16 14 PWM
: bit4out 10 2a cset ; \ set bit 4 to be an output / IN0 8 20 25 13 O1
: bit4h 10 29 cset ; \ set bit 4 to HIGH level / IN1 9 21 24 12 O0
: bit4l 10 29 cclr ; \ set bit 4 to LOW level / IN2 10 22 23 11 IN3
variable outv   \ define a variable outv - OUTPUT Variable
: outl outv2 @ 4 lshift 29 c! ; \ define outl to output outv to LEDs
: setoutin 0f 2a cclr ; \ set the Data Direction Register to 4 OUT 4 IN
: enres 0f 2f cset ; \ now enable the 4 internal resistors on IN lines
: set4in 0f 29 cset ; \ confirm that the bits 0 to 3 are set to IN
: init3 00 2e c! f0 2a c! 0f 2f cset 0f 29 cset ; \ the same as word INIT
: 4shiftl3 4 lshift 0f or ; \ shift 4 IN bits 4x left to position OUT bits

```
: intoout  init begin 28 c@ 4shiftl 29 c! key? until ;  \ show IN on OUT bits
: delay begin dup ms 80 29 cset dup ms 80 29 cclr key? until drop ;  \ x delay
\ 100 delay  ok
: dit 80 29 cset 300 ms 80 29 cclr 100 ms ;  \ morse code short, 100ms
: daa 80 29 cset 900 ms 80 29 cclr 100 ms ;  \ morse code long,  300ms
: sp 300 ms ;                    \ short pause,    100ms
: lp 1100 ms ;                   \ long pause,    1100ms
: MorseSOS  begin dit dit dit sp daa daa daa sp dit dit dit lp key? until ;
: ToSC  decimal begin 1 . 1000 ms key? until ;  \ send 1 to display, 1 per sec
\ tosc 1 1 1 1 1 1 1 1 1 1 1 1  ok
\ MiniDebugger
: ???  hex 2e @ . 2a @ .  28 @ . outv @ . 29 @ . base @ >r hex .s r> base ! ;
\      0    F0    FF    77    FF              <1> -3E22 ok –
\      GPIO  DDR   INPUTS OUTv   OUTl            STACK
\ displays the registers GPIO  DDR  INPUTs variable OUTV LEDs and Stack

\ ExMark – Juergen Pintaske – www.exemark.com –
```

12 – Forth for the BBC micro:bit – Mecrisp Forth

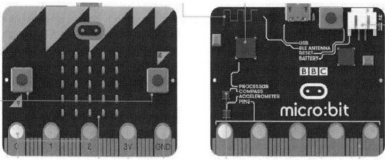

There was an opportunity to have early access to a spare BBC micro:bit.
Matthias Koch took the time and effort to adapt his Mecrsip-Stellaris Forth
to the BBC micro:bit hardware.
Additional micro:bit information in the eBook and book translation I made
https://www.amazon.co.uk/BBC-Micro-Tests-Tricks-Secrets/dp/1541200721/ref=asap_bc?ie=UTF8

And more on Burkhard Kainka's website
http://www.elektronik-labor.de/Microbit/BBCmicro.html
The complete Mecrisp Github File System contains many files covering the
different Controllers it runs on – but which are not necessarily related to the
micro:bit.
We want to make it easy to get to the stage of running the first Forth code
on the micro:bit.

As result here a Starter Pack.
Suggestions to improve it are welcome.

How do you install Mecrisp onto the micro:bit?

1. The Serial Interface needs to link with TeraTerm[1] software making the
   PC a display and keyboard for the micro:bit. Make shure you installed
   TeraTerm. Now get the Starter Pack with:

2. The Mecrisp Forth hex file to throw into the microbit folder on the PC for programming the micro:bit.
3. A small example VFXTESTAPPbit.f ASCII file adapted to the existing Microbit Mecrisp Hex File,
4. The same VFXTESTAPPbit file as Doc for own documentation and extension.
5. More documentation about the small VFXTESTAPP Forth starting example for PC just using 35 Forth Words with explanations can be found here.
6. And you can try the VFXTESTAPP example on the PC without any micro:bit by just downloading and starting the vfxtestapp.exe
7. micro:bit IO Connection Documentation generated by Matthias Koch as there are no official schematics.

More I/O Discussions about the micro:bit in English and as well available in German (not including Forth but a lot of IO information) as supporting information and part of the Forth Bookshelf is here.

Have fun trying it out and feedback for additions and improvements can be sent to Juergen Pintaske at epldfpga@aol.com

Documents
Hardware – All the bits and pieces that make up your BBC micro:bit.
All the BBC micro:bit pins

More details about your BBC micro:bit : Specs & Schematic.
Inofficial Schematic (PDF) – no warranty for correctness and completeness.
N

Not included in the Starter Pack – TeraTerm download (Heise 2017)

13 – Minimal Invasive Serial Connection – A 3 Word Forth Interface

A 3-INSTRUCTION FORTH FOR EMBEDDED SYSTEMS WORK

Illustrated on the Motorola MC68HC11   by Frank Sergeant   Copyright 1991 Frank Sergeant

http://pygmy.utoh.org/forth.html

ABSTRACT

How many instructions does it take to make a Forth for target development work? Does memory grow on trees? Does the cost of the development system come out of your own pocket? A 3- instruction Forth makes Forth affordable for target systems with very limited memory. It can be brought up quickly on strange new hardware. You don't have to do without Forth because of memory or time limitations. It only takes 66 bytes for the Motorola MC68HC11. Full source is provided.

Literary Justifications

I come to Forthifize the 68HC11 not to praise it.
 Had we but memory enough and time,
    this wastefulness, Programmer, were no crime.
The embedded system box is a private place and fine,
    but none should there, I think, megabyte ROMs enshrine.

Do You Want Forth on the Target Board?

Yes. In a FORML paper, it seems reasonable to assume you do want Forth on the target board, if possible, if you can afford it. Without Forth, maybe without a monitor ROM of any sort, you might find yourself in this position: You have to write some code, burn it into an EPROM, guess why it doesn't work, make changes to your code, burn another EPROM ... and do this over and over until something begins to work. Finally you get an LED to flash and your non- programmer friends wonder why you are so excited over such a little thing! You say there's got to be an easier way and start to wish you could afford expensive development systems.

But how do you **put** Forth on the target? If you write your own, you might find yourself in that same situation as you burn EPROMs and wonder why the Forth doesn't run. If you buy one, it might not work with your hardware configuration, it might be too expensive, it might not include full source. You might not have **time** to do all this before starting on your real project. The end product might not be able to afford the PCB space, ROM, and RAM that a Forth requires.

Let's Design the Simplest Possible Forth

Might there be a way to make a very small Forth? How much of the burden can we offload to the host system and what is the minimum that must be done in the target? We are used to the idea of the host providing text editing and source storage services. Let's see if it can also provide all the high-level code while the target provides only the primitives.

The absolute minimum the target must do, it seems to me, is fetch a byte, store a byte, and call a subroutine. Everything else can be done in high-level Forth on the host. (I'm assuming the host and target are connected over a serial line, and that sending and receiving serial bytes will be included as part of accomplishing the three primitive functions.) With those three primitives, memory can be inspected and altered, new routines can be downloaded, and the new routines can be executed. Let's call this a 3-instruction Forth. "Everything else being the same," a 3-instruction Forth should be pretty easy to write and pretty easy to debug. Let's start with a pseudocode description:

Pseudocode

1. Initialize the processor.
2. Initialize the serial port.
3. Repeat the following forever:
   Get a byte from the serial port.
   If byte = 01 [fetch]
     A. Get address from the serial port.

B. Fetch the byte from that address.

C. Send the byte to the serial port.

Else If byte = 02 [store]

A. Get address from the serial port.

B. Get a byte from the serial port.

C. Store the byte at that address.

Else If byte = 03 [call]

A. Get address from the serial port.

B. Jump to the subroutine at that address.

End If.

Step 1 and 2 include whatever housekeeping tasks are needed to set up the processor and the serial port such as initializing the stack and selecting various modes. These steps are particularly simple on the 'HC11. When it wakes up in its bootstrap mode, an internal ROM sets up the stack, turns on the serial port, and waits for a program to be downloaded over the serial line. On the 'HC11, step 1 consists of establishing addressability of the internal registers and ports. This is done by loading Register X with the base address of the register space. The 'HC11's serial out line wakes up in the "wire-or" mode. The only thing we have to do for Step 2 is to un-wire-or it. Doing so eliminates the necessity of putting a pullup resistor on that pin.

In the main part of the routine (step 3), the functions of getting a byte or getting an address from the serial port are required in a number of places, thus they are good candidates for subroutines. Indeed, getting an address can make use of the get a byte subroutine. A byte is sent back to the host in only one place, so there is no point in making that into a subroutine.

Philosophy?

Yes, we could eliminate that last instruction and still be able to set and examine all of the target's RAM and registers. Unfortunately we wouldn't be able to test actual code on the target. With only two instructions (fetch and store) we could exercise the devil out of the hardware, but we really need that third instruction (call) in order to extend the Forth. Thus, I would not be entirely happy to call it Forth with only the first two instructions.

Is it fair to call it a Forth even with all three instructions? After all, it lacks a data stack, headers, either the inner or the outer interpreter (I vacillate on this). It relies on the host (but, then, which target Forth boards connected to a PC over a serial line do not rely on their hosts to at least some extent?). It is extensible and even the main loop can be extended to test for codes in addition to 01, 02, and 03. So, is it a Forth or not?

I lean toward "yes." It has the Forth attributes of simplicity, economy, and (I hope) elegance. What, though, about linking together calls to earlier routines in order to build later routines? The most obvious approach is to build simple assembly language routines on the host and download them to the target one at a time and test them.

Then download higher level assembly routines that call those earlier ones. This is the most memory efficient approach. If you do have extra RAM available on the system then you can use the 3-instruction Forth to build and test a full Forth, and then use it. Either way, starting with a 3-instruction Forth you get to work in an interactive, Forth-like environment.

Can We Afford It?

"But wait," you say, "the 68HC11 has only 192 bytes of onboard RAM (or 256 or 512, depending on the version) -- surely it's not big enough for a Forth or any other monitor!" No, not for a conventional monitor or a conventional Forth. However, it's got memory to spare for a 3-instruction Forth, and that's all we need.

This 3- instruction Forth for the 'HC11 only takes 66 bytes on the target. It was created with Pygmy Forth running on a PC. Following the source code listing is a listing of the actual 66 bytes of 'HC11 machine language, so you should be able to use it with any Forth running on any host. An old slow PC is adequate; no fast, expensive development system is required.

Once that tiny program is running you can use it to do everything else you need. This technique works with all micros, but it is especially easy with the Motorola 68HC11 family. The first reason is that I'm including a listing of the program right here. If you are not using an 'HC11 then you'll have to write an equivalent program for another micro. The second reason is the 'HC11's lovely serial boot loader mode. This eliminates the EPROM burning stage and lets you download the monitor over the serial line.

The 68HC11 gives you another bonus. In the bootstrap mode, the internal ROM initializes the chip and turns on the built-in serial port. With another micro you'll need to write your own code to do this step. If the micro does not have an on-board serial port you'll need to add one, either externally with a serial or parallel port chip, or with on- board I/O lines.

Distributed Development

The 3 instructions are

```
XC@         fetch a byte
XC!         store a byte
XCALL       jump to a subroutine
```

This is a "tokenized" Forth. The host sends a single byte code to the 68HC11. The code 01 stands for XC@, the code 02 stands for XC!, the code 03 stands for XCALL, and any other code is ignored. When the host wants to read a byte it first sends the 01 code to indicate an XC@ instruction and then sends two more bytes to tell the 68HC11 which address should be read. Upon receiving the 01 code the 68HC11 executes the XC@ instruction, which collects the two byte address, reads the byte at that address, and sends the value to the host. The XC! instruction works similarly. The host sends the 02 code followed by two bytes for the address and one byte for the value to be stored.

For the XCALL instruction the host sends the 03 code followed by two bytes for the address. Using the XC! instruction you can download short subroutines for testing, or long programs if the target has enough RAM, or you can program the onboard EEPROM or EPROM if present. Once the routine is downloaded, the host can send the XCALL instruction to cause the 68HC11 to jump to the newly downloaded routine. If the routine ends with a return instruction (RTS) then control will automatically return to the 3-instruction monitor.

Because all of the 68HC11's status, control, and I/O registers are memory mapped, you can use XC@ & XC! to read and set them as if they were regular memory. On other micros, you might need more than the 3 instructions if you need to set registers or I/O ports that aren't memory mapped. In that case you might need a 5 or 6-instruction Forth.

Let's Your Forth and My Forth Do Lunch

"Wait another minute," you say, "I'm not going to sit there and type <value> <address> XC! over and over in order to download a program!" No, of course not. You also run Forth on the host and let the host's Forth do all that work for you. You type high-level commands and the host's Forth breaks all the work down into the 3 simple commands the target Forth understands. This is distributed embedded systems development. Some work is done on the host and some on the target. It allows you the full power of Forth and the full power of an interpreter without requiring extensive resources on the target.

By the power of an interpreter I mean you can examine and set registers and memory interactively from the keyboard. This allows you to exercise the hardware directly. This is so much faster and more convenient than writing your whole program, burning an EPROM, and wondering why it doesn't work. This 3-instruction Forth approach gives you the power of a development system for free if you are using the 68HC11 and for cheap if you are using any other micro.

Sample Session

If you can type 003F XC@ . and understand that you've just displayed the value of the 68HC11's byte at address $003F then you know just about everything you need to know.

Here's a sample session:
Let's pretend I've wired the 68HC11 so that port A pin 01 controls an LED. I can't remember whether a 0 or a 1 turns it on and I'm not sure whether it works. I look in the data book and find that address zero is the port A data address. Although the LED only uses a single bit of port A I don't have

anything else connected so I'll just set the whole byte on or off and see what happens.

```
HEX
0  0 XC!      ( the LED goes on)
FF 0 XC!      ( the LED goes off)
```

Now I want to see something more entertaining so I'll write a little Forth program to make the LED flash. A non-Forther might think of this as defining keyboard macros.

```
DECIMAL
: LED-ON  ( -)   0 0 XC! ;
: LED-OFF ( -) $FF 0 XC!  ;
: DELAY ( -)     500 MS      ;
: FLASHES ( # -)   FOR  LED-ON DELAY LED-OFF DELAY NEXT ;
25 FLASHES    ( for about 25 seconds of entertainment)
 or
10000 FLASHES ( for nearly 3 hours of boredom)
```

MS stands for miliseconds and kills time, thus 500 MS kills about 1/2 a second. If you don't have that word in your Forth system, you can define it with something like
```
: MS  FOR    2000 FOR  NEXT     NEXT    ;
```
then type 10000 MS and see if it takes about 10 seconds. If not, retype the definition of MS with a larger or smaller number than 2000 until you get it close enough.

Note that all of the above definitions are in the host's dictionary, not the target's. They take up no room at all in the target's memory. Only the 3 instructions (which we invoke with the host instructions XC@, XC!, & XCALL) are present in the target's memory.

The Code
The following code loads under Pygmy Forth running on an PC to create a memory image on the PC of the 3- instruction Forth to be run on the 68HC11. It assumes a 68HC11 assembler has already been loaded on top of Pygmy.

3-instruction Forth monitor for 'HC11

(name the 'HC11's serial communication registers)
    $2E CONSTANT SCSR (addr of 'HC11's SCI Status Register)
    $2F CONSTANT SCDR (addr of 'HC11's SCI Data Register)

(provide labels for the two subroutines)
    VARIABLE 'GET-BYTE
    VARIABLE 'GET-ADDR

(how many bytes long is the 3-instruction Forth?)
    VARIABLE MONITOR-LENGTH

(define two 'HC11 assembly language macros)
    : GET-BYTE, (-) 'GET-BYTE @ BSR, ;
    : GET-ADDR, (-) 'GET-ADDR @ BSR, ;

(create the 3-instr Forth)
  CODE MONITOR   (do NOT execute this word on the PC)
    CLRA, CLRB, XGDX, (now X points to base of registers)
    CLRA, $28 ,X STA, (un wire-or port D)

  (define 2 subroutines)
  NEVER, IF, (branch around the 2 subroutines)

   (get-byte) HERE 'GET-BYTE !
   HERE SCSR ,X $20 BRCLR, (wait for incoming char)
          SCDR ,X LDA, (read serial port)
               RTS, (byte is in register A)

   (get-addr) HERE 'GET-ADDR !
            GET-BYTE,
               TAB, (1st byte in Reg B)
            GET-BYTE, (2nd byte in Reg A)
               XGDY, (transfer to Reg Y)
               RTS, (addr is in register Y)

THEN,

```
( start the endless main loop)
BEGIN,
  GET-BYTE,   ( get command code of either 1, 2, or 3)
  1 #, CMPA, 0=, IF,
    ( instruction XC@ was requested)
            GET-ADDR,
            0 ,Y LDA,
    HERE  SCSR ,X  $80 BRCLR, ( wait for Transmit)
                        ( Data Register Empty)
            SCDR ,X  STA, ( send byte to PC)
  ELSE,
  2 #, CMPA, 0=, IF,
    ( instruction XC! was requested)
            GET-ADDR,
            GET-BYTE,
            0 ,Y STA,
  ELSE,
  3 #, CMPA, 0=, IF,
    ( instruction XCALL was requested)
            GET-ADDR,
            0 ,Y JSR,
  THEN, THEN, THEN,
  NEVER, UNTIL,  ( branch back to beginning of main loop)
END-CODE

( calculate how long the 3-instruction Forth is)
HERE ' MONITOR - MONITOR-LENGTH !
```

In order to load the above you must have an 'HC11 assembler running on your PC. You can download such an assembler from the Forth roundtable on GEnie -- do a search in the files section for 68HC11. However, the whole point of the above code is to create the 66 byte image of the 3- instruction Forth. Here is a hex dump of those 66 bytes:

```
0000    4F 5F 8F 4F A7 28 20   F  1F 2E 20 FC A6 2F 39 8D
0010    F7 16 8D F4 18 8F 39 8D  EF 81  1 26   D 8D F0 18
0020    A6  0 1F 2E 80 FC A7 2F  20 16 81  2 26  9 8D DF
0030    8D D6 18 A7  0 20  9 81   3 26  5 8D D2 18 AD  0
0040    20 D5
```

It would be a simple matter to comma those 66 bytes directly into your host Forth, and thus not require the 'HC11 assembler. Although, surely you'd want the assembler for other work you'd do on the 'HC11, wouldn't you? Something like

```
HEX
CREATE MONITOR
   4F C, 5F C, 8F C, 4F C, A7 C,   ...   20 C, D5 C,
```

would serve to build the memory image. Or, you could toss all the numbers on the stack, copy them to the return stack (to retrieve the first bytes first), and do all the comma- ing in a loop, as in

```
DECIMAL
VARIABLE MONITOR-LENGTH     66 MONITOR-LENGTH !
: COMMA-THEM-IN ( ... -)
   66 FOR POP SWAP PUSH PUSH NEXT   (   ) ( rs: ... )
            ( now the bytes are on the return stack)
   66 FOR POP POP C, PUSH NEXT   (   ) ( rs:   )
                ( now the bytes are in memory)   ;


HEX
4F 5F 8F 4F A7 28 20   F  1F 2E 20 FC A6 2F 39 8D
F7 16 8D F4 18 8F 39 8D  EF 81  1 26   D 8D F0 18
A6  0 1F 2E 80 FC A7 2F  20 16 81  2 26  9 8D DF
8D D6 18 A7  0 20  9 81   3 26  5 8D D2 18 AD  0
20 D5  ( put the 66 bytes on the data stack)
```

CREATE MONITOR
   COMMA-THEM-IN

Downloading

Either way you do it, the next step is to download that image to the 'HC11. The following words are defined on the host to allow the 3-instruction Forth to be downloaded to the 'HC11.

```
.OUT    ( a # -) copies a string to the 'HC11.
?EMIT  ( c -)    emits a character if it is displayable,
                 else prints its ASCII value.
.OUTE ( a # -) copies the string to the 'HC11
                 and displays the 'HC11's echo.
?HEX   ( -)      emits hex value of any waiting
                 serial characters.
DL     ( -)      downloads the 3-instruction Forth
                 to the 'HC11.


: .OUT ( a # -)  FOR DUP C@ SER-OUT 1+ NEXT DROP ;

: ?EMIT ( c -) DUP $20 $7F BETWEEN IF EMIT ELSE . THEN ;

: .OUTE ( a # -)
  FOR DUP C@ SER-OUT   SER-IN ?EMIT  1+ NEXT DROP ;
: ?HEX ( -) BASE @ HEX
    BEGIN SER-IN? WHILE SER-IN 3 U.R REPEAT BASE ! ;

: DL ( -)  ( download the 3-instruction Forth)
  $FF SER-OUT  ( tell 'HC11 to pay attention)
  ['] MONITOR ( a)  MONITOR-LENGTH @  ( a #)
  .OUT 1000 FOR NEXT ?HEX      ;
```

Using the Three Primitives

Once the 3-instruction Forth has been downloaded to the 'HC11, those primitives can be used from the host. Here are some examples.

FLIP (hhll - llhh) converts Intel byte order to
            Motorola order, and vice-versa.
ADDR-OUT (a -) sends a 16-bit address to the 'HC11 as
            two bytes.
XC@   (a - c) fetches byte from the 'HC11's address a.

XC!   (c a -) stores byte to the 'HC11's address a.

XCALL   (a -)   makes 'HC11 jump to a subroutine at
           address a.

XDUMP   (a - a+16) dumps 16 bytes starting at 'HC11's
           address a.

XDU   (a # - a') shorthand to repeat XDUMP for as
           many lines as you wish.

: FLIP   (hhll - llhh) DUP $100 * SWAP $100 U/ OR ;

: ADDR-OUT (a -) DUP SER-OUT   FLIP SER-OUT   ;

: XC@   (a - c) 1 SER-OUT   ADDR-OUT SER-IN ;

: XC!   (c a -) 2 SER-OUT   ADDR-OUT SER-OUT ;

: XCALL   (a -) 3 SER-OUT ADDR-OUT ;

: XDUMP (a - a')
  HEX CR DUP 4 U.R 2 SPACES (a)
  DUP (a a) 2 FOR
          8 FOR DUP XC@ 3 U.R 1+ NEXT
          SPACE
        NEXT DROP 2 SPACES
 (a) 2 FOR
       8 FOR DUP XC@ DUP $20 $7F WITHIN NOT
          IF DROP $2E THEN EMIT 1+
        NEXT SPACE
      NEXT ;

: XDU (a # - a') FOR ?SCROLL XDUMP NEXT DROP ;

Bibliography

- Harold M. Martin, "Developing a Tethered Forth Model,"   SIGForth, Vol. 2, No. 3.
- Brad Rodriguez, "A Z8 Talker and Host," The Computer Journal, issue 51, July/August, 1991.

14 - Mixed Language Design using Sockpuppet

The MPE Sockpuppet Forth-to-C interface

May 2016 –
Link to all 3 documents:
PR, article, manual with more documentation

Stephen Pelc
MicroProcessor Engineering
133 Hill Lane
Southampton SO15 5AF
England
t: +44 (0)23 8063 1441
e: sfp@mpeforth.com
w: www.mpeforth.com

Abstract

As processors become ever more complex and the software we are asked to write becomes more complex, it takes ever longer to write the basic drivers for an embedded system. A full digital audio chain is vastly more complex than pumping DAC output into an audio amplifier. Silicon vendors provide C libraries to make using their chips easier. Rather than convert these libraries to Forth, MPE now provides a mechanism to call the C library from Forth.

Introduction

For microcomputers such as the Cortex cores and systems, manufacturers are providing software systems based on C libraries to make using their chips easier. Such libraries reduce the requirement for chip documentation at the expense of software documentation. This tendency has increased to the level that C header files include registers undocumented in the chip user manual. The manufacturer's focus has changed from documentation to time-to-first-hello. The penalty is that chips take longer to learn and the documentation has more errors.

The conventional approach to providing support for development boards in Forth has been to manually port the C library sources to Forth. The SockPuppet system takes a different approach by providing an interface solution between Forth and C; the Forth system calls the underlying C libraries. In turn, this allows the details of the hardware to be abstracted away by the C libraries, whilst allowing the Forth system to provide a powerful, uniform and interactive user interface. This MPE code is directly inspired by Robert Sexton's Sockpuppet interface:

https://github.com/rbsexton/sockpuppet

His contribution and permission are gratefully acknowledged.

Interfacing code from programming language to another is usually called "**mixed language programming**". The MPE ARM/Cortex Forth cross-compiler supports Forth calling functions in C or any language that can provide functions that use the AAPCS calling convention. This is an ARM convention documented in IHI0042F aapcs.pdf. Calls with a variable number of parameters (varargs) are not supported.

The example code in both Forth and C is available for the Professional versions of the ARM Cortex cross compiler with automatic code generation of five interface types. The example code provides a simple GUI for an STM32F429I Discovery board using sample C code provided by ST and others. A version for the BBC micro:bit is in preparation. The interface is currently defined for Cortex-M CPUs only. All versions of the compiler can be used with hand-written assembler code.

How the Forth to C interface works

Both Flash and RAM memory are partitioned, one pair for C and the other for Forth. Because of the arcane and undocumented nature of start-up for C compiler target code, the initial boot of the system is performed by the C code in order to make sure that the initialisation is correct.

Every function that is exported from the C world to the Forth world appears as one of a number of types of call. These words are called "externs". You can handcraft these words in
assembler, but the MPE cross compiler compiler includes code generators for several techniques. The call format and return values match the AAPCS standard used by ARM C compilers.

Each calling technique has its own pros and cons. They are discussed in following sections.

• SVC calls. You just need to know the SVC numbers. SVC calls provide the greatest isolation between sections of code written in other languages. The functions foreign to Forth are accessed by SVC calls and/or jump tables. The example solution uses SVC calls for most foreign functions. Regardless of the call technique used by the majority of your code, all techniques rely on a small number of SVC calls.

• Jump table. The base address of the table can be set at run time, e.g. by making a specific SVC call. The calling words fetch the run-time address from the table, given an index. This technique has good performance and few problems.

• Double indirect call. A primary jump table is at a fixed address and contains the addresses of secondary tables, which hold the actual routine addresses. The fixed address and both indices must be known at compile time. This technique is used by TI's Stellaris and some NXP parts to access driver code in ROM.

• Direct calls to the address of the routine. You need to know the address at compile time.

There is a practical limit of four arguments if you use SVC calls for the insulation between Forth and C because Cortex CPUs automatically stack four registers for an interrupt. The other interface methods do not suffer from this limit. It is a matter of convention between the Forth and C code as to parameter passing order. It can be changed by either side. MPE convention is for the left-most Forth parameter to be passed in R0. This matches the AAPCS code used by the hosted Forth compilers such as VFX Forth for ARM Linux.

SVC calls
The examples use the MPE calling convention and are illustrated in assembler as well as by using the code generator. The code generator interface is much to be preferred and preserves far more of the information in the C prototype. The decision to use the C prototype is deliberate and follows long-established practice in MPE's hosted systems.

SVC(67) void BSP_LCD_DrawCircle(int x, int y, int r);
\ SVC 67: draw a circle of radius r at position (x,y).

The code generator parses the extern definition above and generates the extern as a function with three parameters implemented as SVC call 67. If you really want to demonstrate your assembler prowess, the code below performs the same operation.

```
CODE BSP_LCD_DrawCircle \ x y r --
\ SVC 67 draw a circle of radius r at position (x,y).
  mov r2, tos                           \ r
  ldr r1, [ psp ], # 4                  \ y
  ldr r0, [ psp ], # 4                  \ x
  svc # __SAPI_BSP_LCD_DrawCircle
  ldr tos, [ psp ], # 4                 \ restore TOS
  next,
END-CODE
```

When the SVC call occurs, the Cortex CPU stacks registers R0-R3, R12, LR, PC, xPSR on the calling R13 stack with R0 at the lowest address. The SVC handler places the address of this frame in R0/R4, extracts the SVC call number, reloads the AAPCS parameters from the frame and jumps to the appropriate C function. In this case

```
void BSP_LCD_DrawCircle(
  uint16_t Xpos, uint16_t Ypos, uint16_t Radius
);
```

SVC calls provide the highest insulation between Forth and C, but suffer from several issues.

•The SVC call mechanism is part of the Cortex interrupt and exception system. The assembler and/or C side of this uses code written in assembler to allow the C routines called from a jump table to to be AAPCS compliant.

•The SVC mechanism is inefficient compared to a direct AAPCS handler.

•Because SVC calls are part of the CPU interrupt mechanism, you have to care how long a call takes. Playing games with the Cortex interrupt mechanism can fix this, but is complex.

Jump table

In order to avoid the run-time penalties of the SVC call mechnism, you can make an array of function pointers in C or assembler and call functions using an index into the table.

```
jumptable:
dd func0 ; address of function 0
dd func1 ; address of function 1
 ..
```

We still need to know the address of the jump table. This is found using an SVC call (15) and stored in a variable. The jump table address could be hard-coded, but given the horrors of perverting link map files and the like, the overhead of a single SVC call is preferable.

```
SVC( 15 ) void * GetDirFnTable( void );
\ Returns the address of the jump table.
variable JT \ -- addr
\ Holds the address of the jump table.
JT holdsJumpTable
\ Tell cross compiler where jump table address is held.
: initJTI \ -- ; initialise jump table calls
  GetDirFnTable JT ! ;
JTI( n ) int open(
  const char * pathname, int flags, mode_t mode
);
```

If constructed in assembler, the SVC despatch table and the main jump table can be the same
table; it's just a question of what you put in the table.

Double indirect call tables

Some vendors, particularly TI, use a table of tables approach. The sub-tables provide the API for a particular peripheral, e.g. UARTs. Before use, you have to declare the base address of the primary ROM table used for calling ROM functions. For Luminary/TI CPUs, this will probably be:

```
$0100:0010 setPriTable
```

Now you can define a set of ROM calls, for example, again for a TI CPU.

```
DIC( 4, 0 ) void ROM_GPIOPinWrite(
  uint32 ui32Port, uint8 ui8Pins, uint8 ui8Val
);
```

where:

- ROM_APITABLE is an array of pointers located at 0x0100.0010.
- ROM_GPIOTABLE is an array of pointers located at ROM_APITABLE[4].

- ROM_GPIOPinWrite is a function pointer located at ROM_GPIOTABLE[0].

Parameters:
- ui32Port is the base address of the GPIO port.
- ui8Pins is the bit-packed representation of the pin(s).
- ui8Val is the value to write to the pin(s).

To call this function, use the Forth form:

```
port pins val ROM_GPIOPinWrite
```

Direct calls
Where the address of the routine is known at the Forth compile time, you can use a direct call.

DIR(addr) int foo(int a, char *b, char c);

The Forth word marshalls the parameters and calls the subroutine at target address addr.

Extracting information from C
It is convenient to have a certain amount of information available from the C portion of the code. This is supported by a few SVC calls that exist in all versions of the Sockpuppet API.

svc(0) int SAPI-Version(void);
SVC 00: Return the version of the API in use.
svc(1) int GetSharedVars(void);
SVC 01: Get the address of the shared variable list.
svc(15) int GetSvcFnTable(void);
SVC 15: Get the address of the SVC function table.

In order to support data sharing between C and Forth, the C can export named objects which can appear as Forth words.

C Linkage structure

```
#define DYNLINKNAMEMLEN 22
typedef struct {
// This union is a bit crazy, but it's the simplest way of
// getting the compiler to shut up.
union {
void (*fp) (void);
int* ip;
unsigned int ui;
unsigned int* uip;
unsigned long* ulp;
} p;                    //< Pointer to the object of interest (4)
int16_t size; //< Size in bytes (6)
int16_t count;          //< How many (8)
int8_t kind; //< Is this a variable or a constant? (9)
uint8_t strlen;         //< Length of the string (10)
const char name[DYNLINKNAMEMLEN]; //<Null-Term C string.
} runtimelink_t;
```

When the Forth system powers up it runs the Forth word **dy-populate** which uses SVC call 01 to get the address of the **dynamiclinks[]** table, and walks through the table creating Forth named variables whose addresses match those in the C system. A Forth word **dy-show** is provided to list the entries in the table.

Forth Linkage structure

```
interpreter
: hword 2 field ;
: byte 1 field ;
target
struct /runtimelink \ -- len
\ Forth equivalent of the C structure above.
  int fdy.val        \ usually a pointer 0, 4
  hword fdy.size          \ size in bytes 4, 2
  hword fdy.count    \ how many 6, 2
  byte fdy.type           \ variable or constant 8, 1
  byte fdy.nlen           \ name length 9, 1
  22 field fdy.zname      \ zero terminated name 10, 22
```

```
end-struct
```

The accessor words just read the fields defined above. They are defined as compiler macros. For interaction on the target, use the field names above.

Compiler

```
: dy.val fdy.val @ ;                    \ addr -- n
: dy.size fdy.size w@ ;      \ addr -- w
: dy.count fdy.count w@ ;  \ addr -- w
: dy.type fdy.type c@ ;     \ addr -- c
: dy.name fdy.nlen ;                    \ addr -- addr'
target
```

A set of support words allow us to run down the table and create Forth **VALUE**s and **CONSTANT**s.

Demonstration code

In order to evaluate the Sockpuppet technique and to provide a demonstration environment we decided to port the MPE PowerView GUI code to an STM32F429I Discovery board, which includes a small QVGA colour panel.

We made a decision to standardise on the gcc compiler maintained by ARM:
 https://launchpad.net/gcc-arm-embedded
This seems to be a clean compiler, but it has a few deficiencies:
- It does not include a make utility,
- Every silicon vendor ships a different version of Eclipse with different make tools,
- They are all incompatible.

A good alternative for supported hardware is the online mbed compiler:
 https://developer.mbed.org/
The alternative is just to take the silicon vendor's "free" tools, accepting that we will need a huge amount of disc space (almost free these days) and a degree of pain in learning the tool-chain. The days when you could just download and go are long past. Whatever you do, there will be pain.

Conclusions
Mixed language programming for embedded systems is entirely feasible and productive.

Do not assume that the C libraries provided by the silicon vendors are bug-free.

You can use the Forth to debug the C.

Once you have set it up, it all works surprisingly well, but compared to Forth cross-compilation, the C compilation chain is baroque.

Using the C libraries for hardware access saves a huge amount of time reading chip documentation. As the use of silicon vendor C libraries increases, silicon vendor are placing less importance on correct documentation. We have already found devices whose C libraries depend on undocumented registers.

Acknowledgements
Robert Sexton is responsible for the ideas and implementation of Sockpuppet. His dedication has made it a production-grade environment.

Elizabeth Rather convinced me long ago of the necessity of good notations. This convinced us to port the extern interface from hosted systems to the cross-compiler.

15 - v4th – An Approach using Forth Techniques

[feb 2017]

What is v4th?

v4th is a Forth-like programming platform/framework for embedded microcontrollers. Much like Forth and LISP derivatives, it provides another "secret weapon" in the savvy programmer's arsenal/toolkit/bag-of-tricks.

Since its first version on the RCA 1802, v4th has been used to build many successful products, and ported to a wide variety of CPUs over the years, with continuous evolution and improvements.
Today, versions exist for MSP430, MIPS, RX, and various flavors of ARM targets.

v4th is not Forth -- not quite. It only runs an "inner interpreter" threading engine, and thus has no interactive REPL console, native compiler, nor its own IDE.

Then why use it?

High Performance. v4th's speed is in the same league as the very best fully-compiled Forths or C, along with a very compact code size footprint. Note that v4th was developed not for the mere ego-gratification of offering Yet Another Forth, but to fulfill a real need that classic Forths cannot.

Just like Forth, v4th uses a dual-stack Virtual Machine and nested definitions, and allows you to use the same design methodology and programming techniques as Forth. The author finds it much more productive and less annoying than C.

v4th is intended for embedded turnkey systems that are purpose-built machines, where user-programmability is undesirable and inappropriate.

Nevertheless v4th is completely "open"; an experienced MCU jockey can easily modify the software at will.

In the hands of a savvy programmer, v4th can easily produce high-quality results similar to Forth Inc.'s SwiftX or MPEforth's VFX. Forth programmers (especially those with assembly-language experience) have no trouble grokking v4th's idioms. It is in fact an assembly language package that rides on top of the assembler, and thus provides all the convenient and productive features that modern developers expect.

This actually has some advantages:

(caveat: we are now into nerdy technicalities that will make the most sense to people who are familiar with Forth internals.)

- extremely compact footprints are possible; apps can be built within (for instance) 256 bytes of ROM and 16 bytes of RAM. There is no dictionary structure, so all v4th words are headerless.

- transparent access to the datasheet's standardized symbols; there is no need for a lot of 'constant' declarations; the assembler already knows the vendor's standardized labels (e.g. for the UART's baud-rate-divisor register), because the vendor has already pre-supplied the appropriate header files that contain the necessary #define and/or EQU directives. It's a nice thing, when your symbols agree with the manufacturer's documentation.

- inherits the assembler's IDE, with all those nifty features, and all the JTAG debug amenities that the assembler provides.

- WYWIWYG debugging; there is no doubt about what machine code will execute, because What You Wrote Is What You Get. There is no compiler that makes any (perhaps unexpected) decisions on your behalf.

- very high performance; v4th is single-indirect (aka "direct-threaded"), and (depending on the target CPU) can often use a one-instruction NEXT. The v4th nucleus is practically guaranteed to remain resident in caches.

- highly optimized primitives; v4th provides state-of-the-art efficiency; needless stack-pumping is eliminated.
  - non-destructive variants that obviate 'dup' and 'over'.
  - reversed variants that obviate 'swap'.
  - fully conjugated conditionals, e.g. 'nif' instead of "not if".
  - multi-way and table-based branches for state-machine designs.
  - branch target addresses are absolute, not relative offsets; thus no calculation cycles are required.
  - ToS (and typically also NoS) are cached in CPU registers, instead of being held in RAM.
  - high-level inline literals that use scratchpad registers, instead of the parameter stack. e.g. "addk, 5" instead of "5 +"; "strva, VALUE, ADDR" instead of "VALUE ADDR !"; wasteful push/pop thrashing is eliminated; for example, Forth's

```
Daddr @ PIXSIZE CHARWIDTH * - Daddr !
```

is

```
DW  pstrkk,-(PIXSIZE * CHARWIDTH),Daddr
```

in v4th's idiom, and (of course) runs much faster.

- low-level inline macros that eliminate nesting; many v4th words have both inline and "worded" cognates, e.g. for ARM (note the upper-/lower-case difference):

<pre>
<code>

```
NEXT      MACRO
          ldr     PC, [i], #4
          ENDM
```

```
DUP        MACRO
           str      n, [p, #-4]!
           mov      n, t
           ENDM

dup        DUP
           NEXT
```

Here is v4th's NEXT for some other targets:

MSP430:
```
mov       @i+, PC
```

RX:
```
RTS        ;  the UserStackPointer is hijacked,
           ;  and used as the Interpreter Pointer.
```

RX again, with an alternate implementation for the meek and timid:
```
mov.l     [i+], w
jmp       w
```

MIPS:
```
lw   w, 0(i)
jr   w
addi i, i, #4          ; executed in branch delay-slot.
```

```
</code>
</pre>
```

- utterly flexible; because v4th words are all in assembly language, you can quite seamlessly switch to/from writing in machine code and high-level, on the fly. This point deserves a bit of amplification: Forth is not a perfect language, and some jobs (e.g. DSP or graphics) can become awkward and klunky. v4th allows you to completely bypass the Forth Virtual Machine, and take full advantage of the CPU's general-purpose register set and complete instruction repertoire.

Lastly, v4th is interoperable with C; you can take advantage of existing middleware such as USB drivers or TCP/IP protocols (like it or not, they're probably implemented in C), without re-inventing the wheel.

As a comparative example, here are three ways of flashing an LED:
(the LED blinks quickly at first, then slows down)

<pre>
<code>

in Forth:
----

literal1 constant LEDPORT
literal2 constant LEDBIT


```
: toggleLED              \ read/modify/write, toggle LEDBIT only
LEDPORT @                \ get LED status
dup not                  \ toggle status
LEDBIT and               \ isolate bit
swap LEDBIT not and      \ clear LED bit
or LEDPORT !             \ merge new status, and update port
;
```


\ : toggleLED LEDPORT @ dup not LEDBIT and swap LEDBIT not and or LEDPORT ! ;
\ this one-line version is bad style, but it's fun to say the words out loud...
:-)

```
: LEDflash
0
begin
 1 + dup              \ increment delay
 begin
  1 - dup 0=
 until
 drop toggleLED
again
;
```

in v4th:

```
LEDPORT EQU        AsmSymbolForPortReg
LEDBIT  EQU        AsmSymbolForPortPin


 NEST    toggleLED            ; 'NEST' is v4th's equivalent of 'DOCOL'.
         DW atk, LEDPORT, nott, rmwam, LEDPORT, LEDBIT       ;
read/modify/write
                             using inline address and mask.
         DW   nexit           ; 'nexit' is v4th's equivalent of 'SEMIS'.


 NEST    LEDflash
         DW        zero
         DW        begin
         DW         inc, dup ;  increment delay
         DW         begin
         DW          dec
         DW         zuntiln  ; v4th's equivalent of "dup 0= until"
         DW         drop, toggleLED
         DW         again
; infinite loop, so 'nexit' is not required
```

using v4th inline machine-code macros:

```
LEDflash
          ZERO
_flashloop
          INC          ; increment delay
          DUP
_delayloop
          DEC
          bnz          _delayloop

          DROP
          ATK          LEDPORT
          NOTT
          RMWAM  LEDPORT, LEDBIT          ; read/modify/write,
                                          ; toggle LEDBIT only
          b            _flashloop

</code>
</pre>
```

And of course, for those instances where normal v4th may not be the most appropriate means of solving the problem, you can still write a v4th word as fully-handcrafted assembly code, and that word is added to the vocabulary like any other.

Finally, I must give my sincere thanks and acknowledgement to all the fine Forth folks who have helped me with v4th's evolution and improvement over the years. There are too many people to list here, but I hope that they all know who they are...

I'm somewhat clever, but really it has been other people's feedback and input to v4th that makes me look more brilliant.   :-)

Two people deserve special mention:

1 - My brother Myron Plichota; he is brilliant.
2 - I feel truly honored that Cyde W. Philips Jr. (another brilliant fellow) has seen fit to incorporate some v4th constructs into his recent FISH forth.

cheers,   - vic
vic plichota
embedded systems architect

vic.plichota@gmail.com   vic@MachineQuiltingRobot.com
voicemail: 1 254 247 2265
mobile/text 1 254 913 9149 (please pre-arrange)
email to mobile/text 2549139149 (@ "at") mms (."dot") att (."dot") net
Skype   vapats1802   Kik   vapats
https://www.linkedin.com/in/vicplichota
https://www.dropbox.com/sh/grnt4bb34och0jd/AABuuZ71ZkiIbfrv_QwpyG
Vwa?dl=0
http://MachineQuiltingRobot.com/

—
antares technical services - 4403 CR 3841 - San Antonio, TX - USA 7825

16 – Minimum Word Set and Comparison

Paul Bennett, HIDECS

Some discussion has been bubbling in the background since before last year's EuroForth. The problem is seen that, for deeply embedded controls, some words in the CORE are not suitable candidates for inclusion in the system.

If we are to allow a claim of compliance to the standard for such deeply embedded systems we may need to look at a sensible BASE-LINE set of words that we should be able to count on to be there for a system that may connect to the embedded controller via a communications port only, without being over-burdened by words that are only sensible in the desk-top realm.

Hence, trying to establish what words might be included in the Baseline set began via email discussions between a few of us who are more into the small controller markets. This can include 8-bit, 16-bit, 18-bit, 21-bit, and 32-bit processors.

So, the set suggested below is probably richer than an absolute minimalist set would be (that extreme is saved for the Umbilical Only System and may be as little as XC@, XC! and XCALL).

The following 71 words are suggested at this stage. Words for inclusion:

Memory Access:-

HERE	C@	C!	@	,	C,	ALIGN	ALIGNED
CELL	CELLS	CALIGN	CALIGNED	CHAR+	CHARS		
!	'	[']					

Arithmetic:

+	–	2*	*	/	2/
MOD	*/MOD	UM*			

Logic:

0=	0<	0<>	=	<	>
AND	OR	XOR	LSHIFT	RSHIFT	

Stack:

DUP	SWAP	OVER	DROP	>R	R>	R@	ROT

Flow Control:

IF	ELSE	THEN	BEGIN	WHILE	UNTIL	DO
I	J	LOOP	EXECUTE			

Defining:

:	;	CREATE	DOES>	CONSTANT	VARIABLE

I/O:

KEY	KEY?	CR	EMIT

Tools: (\   .S)

Exception Management:	CATCH	THROW
Special Words:	TBD.	

Some special words will have to be added for controllers and FLASH and IO handling.

About The Exception Management Choice:

It has been felt that the Catch & Throw mechanism is the most flexible way of managing exceptions that may arise for different reasons.

The standard gives a range of values pre-defined for specific error types. Minimal action would be the actions of ABORT (-1 or any non-zero code), see Standard reference 6.1.0680.

Some final Words:

It is seen that this smaller set of words, defined as a Baseline Set, would allow simpler starter systems for those who may be confused by the rich dictionary of some of the offerings.

In the deeply embedded controller world it would also assist with preferring a fully certified product for such deeply embedded controllers, while also being able to claim full adherence to a standard.

The observant will realise that IMMEDIATE is not in the list. The need for this rather depends on implementation details and whether or not the IMMEDIATE flag is required in the word's header or not.
Other issues of STATE also come into this category and there have been lengthy discussions on both factors.

Minimum Word Set Comparison
1. Ting   2. Brinkhoff   3. Plichota
4. B16   5. B16 Small   6. GA-F18
7. Proposed Minimum Word Set

Type	Name	Forth 2012 Reference	1	2	3	4	5	6	7
Memory Access	C@	6.1.0870	1	1	1	0	1	0	1
	C!	6.1.0850	1	1	1	0	0	0	1
	@	6.1.0650	1	1	1	0	1	1	1
	!	6.1.0010	1	1	1	0	0	1	1
	HERE	6.1.1650	0	0	0	0	0	0	1
	C,	6.1.0860	0	0	0	0	0	0	1
	,	6.1.0150	0	0	0	0	0	0	1
Math	+	6.1.0120	1	1	1	1	1	1	1
	-	6.1.0160	1	0	0	0	0	1	1
	/	6.1.0230	1	0	0	0	0	0	1
	MOD	6.1.1890	1	0	0	0	0	0	1
	2*	6.1.0320	0	0	0	0	0	1	1
	2/	6.1.0330	0	0	0	0	1	1	1

Category	Word	Ref							
	UM*	6.1.2360	0	0	0	0	0	0	1
Logic	NAND		0	1	1	0	0	0	0
	XOR	6.1.2490	1	0	1	1	1	0	1
	AND	6.1.0720	1	0	0	1	1	1	1
	OR	6.1.1980	1	0	0	1	1	1	1
	LSHIFT	6.1.1805	0	0	0	0	0	0	1
	RSHIFT	6.1.6162	0	0	0	0	0	0	1
Flow Control	IF	6.1.1700	1	1	1	0	0	1	0
	0BRANCH		0	1	0	0	0	0	1
	BEGIN	6.1.0760	1	0	0	0	0	0	1
	AGAIN	6.2.0700	1	0	0	0	0	0	1
	DO	6.1.1240	1	0	1	0	0	0	0
	EXIT	6.1.1380	1	1	0	0	0	0	1
	ELSE	6.1.01310	1	0	0	0	0	0	0
	THEN	6.1.2270	1	0	0	0	0	0	0
	WHILE	6.1.2430	1	0	0	0	0	0	0
	REPEAT	6.1.2120	1	0	0	0	0	0	0
	LOOP	6.1.1800	1	0	0	0	0	0	0
	PAUSE		0	0	0	0	0	0	1
Stack	DUP	6.1.1290	1	0	1	1	1	1	1
	SWAP	6.1.2260	1	0	1	0	0	0	1
	DROP	6.1.1260	1	0	1	1	1	1	1
	NIP	6.2.1930	0	0	0	1	1	0	0
	OVER	6.1.1990	1	0	0	1	1	1	1
	R@	6.1.2070	1	0	0	1	0	0	1
	>R	6.1.0580	1	0	1	1	1	1	1

Category	Word	Ref								
	R>	6.1.2060	1		0	1	1	1	1	1
	.S	15.6.1.0220	0		0	0	0	0	0	1
Defin-ing	:	6.1.0450	1		0	1	0	0	0	1
	;	6.1.0450	1		0	1	0	0	1	1
	CREATE	6.1.1000	0		0	0	0	0	0	1
	CONSTANT	6.1.0950	1		0	0	0	0	0	1
	VARIABLE	6.1.2410	1		0	0	0	0	0	1
I/O	IN		1		1	0	0	0	1	0
	OUT		1		1	0	0	0	0	0
	KEY	6.1.0750	0		0	0	0	0	0	1
	KEY?	10.6.1.1755	0		0	0	0	0	0	1
	EMIT	6.1.1320	0		0	0	0	0	0	1
other	INVERT	6.1.1720	1		0	0	0	0	0	0
	LIT		0		0	1	1	1	0	0
	DODOES		0		1	0	0	0	0	0
	EXECUTE	6.1.1370	1		0	0	1	1	1	1
	DOES>	6.1.1250	0		0	0	0	0	0	1
	C@+		0		0	0	0	1	0	0
	C@.		0		0	0	0	1	0	0
	C!+		0		0	0	0	1	0	0
	C!.		0		0	0	0	1	0	0
	@.		0		0	0	0	1	0	0
	a		0		0	0	1	0	1	0
	@a		0		0	0	0	0	1	0
	A@		0		0	0	1	0	0	0
	A@+		0		0	0	1	0	0	0
	@p		0		0	0	0	0	1	0
	@b		0		0	0	0	0	1	0
	@+		0		0	0	0	1	1	0

!p		0	0	0	0	0	1	0
!+		0	0	0	0	1	1	0
!.		0	0	0	0	1	0	0
!b		0	0	0	0	0	1	0
a!		0	0	0	1	0	1	0
A!+		0	0	0	1	0	0	0
b!		0	0	0	0	0	1	0
AC!		0	0	0	1	0	0	0
AC@+		0	0	0	1	0	0	0
AC!+		0	0	0	1	0	0	0
AC@+		0	0	0	1	0	0	0
>A		0	0	0	1	0	0	0
+C		0	0	0	0	1	0	0
C2/		0	0	0	0	1	0	0
+*		0	0	0	0	0	1	0
*+		0	0	0	1	0	0	0
+C		0	0	0	1	0	0	0
/-		0	0	0	1	0	0	0
R@+		0	0	0	1	0	0	0
RC@		0	0	0	1	0	0	0
RC@+		0	0	0	1	0	0	0
-IF		0	0	0	0	0	1	0
<name> ;		0	0	0	0	0	1	0
<name>		0	0	0	0	0	1	0
unext		0	0	0	0	0	1	0
next		0	0	0	0	0	1	0
RET		0	0	0	1	1	0	0
JZ		0	0	0	1	1	0	0
JNZ		0	0	0	1	1	0	0

	1	2	3	4	5	6	7
JC	0	0	0	1	1	0	0
JNC	0	0	0	1	1	0	0
GZ	0	0	0	1	1	0	0
GNZ	0	0	0	1	1	0	0
GC	0	0	0	1	1	0	0
GNC	0	0	0	1	1	0	0
GOTO	0	0	0	1	1	0	0
LITC	0	0	0	1	1	0	0
data	0	0	0	0	0	1	0
---u	0	0	0	0	0	1	0
--l-	0	0	0	0	0	1	0
--lu	0	0	0	0	0	1	0
-d--	0	0	0	0	0	1	0
-d-u	0	0	0	0	0	1	0
-dl-	0	0	0	0	0	1	0
-dlu	0	0	0	0	0	1	0
r---	0	0	0	0	0	1	0
r-l-	0	0	0	0	0	1	0
r-lu	0	0	0	0	0	1	0
rd--	0	0	0	0	0	1	0
rdl-	0	0	0	0	0	1	0
rdlu	0	0	0	0	0	1	0
CALL	0	0	0	1	1	0	0
JMP	0	0	0	1	1	0	0
RET	0	0	0	1	1	0	0
NOP	0	0	0	1	1	0	0
COM	0	0	0	0	1	0	0
Totals of these Base Word Sets	37	12	18	40	36	47	40

17 – Certifying your Code

Paul E. Bennett [HIDECS Consultancy]

Thorough testing and verification of code is often neglected. Paul Bennett introduces us to concepts and procedures that we can all use and concludes that Forth can be used in most safety critical situations. It has been a long-held belief, within the software industry generally, that the only programmes that are capable of being 100% tested are "Toy" programmes.
I am presuming that this is meant to indicated programmes of under a couple of hundred LOC. Programmes of such a small size would be quite within the realms of any programmer (in whatever language) to fully test in reasonable time. However, let us look at what Forth gives us that is different to many programming environments.

High Integrity Systems, we are assured, have been thoroughly tested. This leaves us all with the unanswered question of "How Thorough is thorough?" Considering that much of the High Integrity software that keep our planes in the sky, run our traffic lights and keep us alive on the operating theatre table are usually many thousands of lines of code can we trust that the testing has been done well enough to give us confidence.
What the hardware sector has that the software sector would probably like to have is the ability to attach a "Certificate of Conformity" that can present tangible proof that the system has been developed and tested in accordance with some auditable standard method.

The software tools industry always seems to be promising that the new whizzo software tool is the "Silver Bullet" we have been seeking. Development suites like Rhapsody (from Ilogix) or SPARK-Ada have been touted as the most logical choice for Safety Critical Systems Development because they are proven correct mathematically. Not only are these tools very expensive they also seem to give an unwelcome boost the resources requirements on the embedded system.

In a recent thread on comp.lang.forth Pete < forthsafe@yahoo.com > asked whether or not Forth could be used in Safety Critical Systems and pass the stringent requirements of FDA or DO178B. As one who has been involved in the development and certification of systems that have had to pass such scrutiny I am happy to say that Forth, produced in the right way, can indeed be used for such projects.

In Forth, each word can be considered as a complete programme in its own right. It may be just a subroutine of a much larger programme but in itself it is quite complete and, at the interpreted level, is interactively available for quite thorough testing. Any Forth word can be considered as a fully single minded simple programme in itself. The ultimate "Toy" programme.
Because Forth words, written properly (preferably with reference to a coding standard), are usually quite small and simple we are merely coupling a number of individual, complete, simple programmes.

Each word constructed using other previously tested words would inherit the properties of testing already carried out. The words in a specific lexicological grouping can be seen as existing between programming surfaces that provide the API between functional entities. In this way, the most complex Forth programmes can carry through the testing at a level thatmore or less trivially accomplished.
The idea of programming surfaces establishes a useful reference for situations where application code is developed away from the real target. So long as the certification can fully prove equivalence there should remain no issues (bar hardware timing) that would invalidate the certification of the software.
It was realising this simple facet of Forth that gave me confidence enough to develop the review and testing process to a method for fully certifying Forth code. The method also works with assembly, so long as the assembly subroutines are small, single function, highly coherent and utilise minimal coupling of the systems the code is being developed for.
It should be obvious that the development process by which High Integrity Software is developed for these Safety Critical Systems should be rigorous, and rigorously applied.

Development Management processes that fall below CMMR level 3 are less likely to be trusted well enough for software certification to be believable. Ideally, the organisation should be at level 4 or 5. Therefore, establishing a decent development process is a necessary pre-requisite to being able to produce certifiable software. It is an absolute necessity that the exact source code that is certified is always uniquely identifiable (name, version, production date, test dates etc). A version control and configuration management system, therefore, becomes essential.

Within this article I have included an arbitrary bit of code which should illustrate how the certification process not only improves the presentation of the code but also ensures its logically correct implementation.
The form format is made part of the source code file along with the words glossary description and any additional notes. The example code is simple enough to follow without the addition of the glossary comments. However, the incorporation of the glossary text within the source files aids fuller understanding without having to reference other sources.

```
\ ************************************************
: .TOS ( S: n1 -- n1 )
( G: Non-destructively print the top of parameter stack item )
( n1 to the current terminal. )
DUP . ;
\ ************************************************
\ *      Inspection      *      Function Test      *      Limits Test      *
\ *                      *                      *                      *
\ *                      *                      *                      *
\ ************************************************

\ ************************************************
: FIB-ALG ( S: n1\n2 -- n2\n3 )
( G: Given two numbers, n1 and n2, of a Fibonacci series )
( calculate the next number, n3, of the series. )
SWAP OVER + ;
\ ************************************************
\ *      Inspection      *      Function Test      *      Limits Test      *
\ *                      *                      *                      *
```

```
\ *                 *                  *                  *
\ ********************************************************************

\ ********************************************************************
: FIBONACCI ( S: n1\n2\limit -- )
( G: Given the two numbers, n1 and n2, of a Fibonacci series )
( calculate and print the succeeding numbers in the series )
( up to limit to the current terminal. )
>R
BEGIN DUP R@ > NOT
WHILE .TOS FIB-ALG
REPEAT 2DROP R> DROP
\ ********************************************************************
\ *     Inspection     *     Function Test     *     Limits Test     *
\ *                    *                       *                     *
\ *                    *                       *                     *
\ ********************************************************************
```

The three boxes underneath the word definition are intended as an appropriate space in which to collect signatures from the code inspection and test personnel. The three boxes deal with a specific aspect of the inspection and tests to be applied.

You can choose whether or not the three boxes are a permanent feature within the source file or generated during documentation print-out. You may even discover a way, within your own configuration management system, to incorporate electronic signatures within these boxes.

Inspection

This is the traditional static inspection run along Fagan Inspection lines. The code inspector should ensure that the code appears to fully implement the requirements stated within the glossary text that is part of the source.

This requires that the inspector will need to ensure that the called words used within this definition are also previously certified. Previous reviews of the glossary text should have, of course, ensured that the intent for the word under examination as defined in the glossary text is right for the application. This is one of the benefits of writing the glossary text first.

Function Test

The function test is the first time that the code is formally run. The code might have been exercised by the programmer immediately after coding but this formal run records the performance of the word in comparison to the intent expressed in the glossary text.

Several occurrences of the function test would be usual, especially with different representative values, to provide a level of confidence that the function always does as is expected. This test only covers the normal operating range.

Limits Test

The Limits test is an opportunity to test the code to beyond the expected normal range of operation. If the code is able to deal with wildly out of bounds input stimuli, high rate call demand (if the code is an interrupt) and still behave in a rational manner then this test can be deemed passed.

In order to perform this test on your code often requires a very inventive frame of mind to ensure that the operation is, as far as is practicable, out of the normal operational range.

With the code having satisfied the test and inspection personnel, their signatures can be attached to the source print-out. This signed listing then needs storing in a long-term archive until the product in which the software exists is no longer in service and an additional five years following its decommissioning.

Programming Surfaces

I have used the term programming surfaces in this article and perhaps now is a good time to explain what they are.

The best description of programming surfaces is perhaps as an interface between underlying machine level code and the application language layer or between the application language layer and the application itself.

This idea of surfaces is very useful for demarcation of the various elements of a system which, if the surfaces can be proven equivalent, allow easy movement of segments of code from one platform to another. This is most useful when the underlying processor platform goes out of production and you need to replace it with another similar item of hardware.

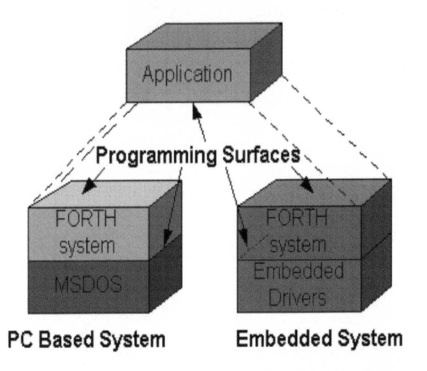

PC Based System   **Embedded System**

So long as the machine-level to application language level interface surfaces are proven equivalent there should be very little problem in making the substitution. This also works on a finer grained level throughout Forth.
Programming surfaces are part of a component oriented approach to system development. Components are a firmer, harder edged form of objects that can be comprehended, tested and proven of sufficiently good quality.

Summary

This technique to certification is very simple to apply and, coupled with a suitably robust version and change management process that tracks modifications of the source code, can lead to the production of fully certifiable code that satisfies the most stringent requirements (DO178B, FDA, CE marking etc.).

Just creating source code that incorporates the inspection boxes is not enough. The code has got to qualify by proper inspection and testing methods being applied. Coverage of testing can easily approach 100% of all statements.

Application of a certification process against coding standards and language specification standards will improve the quality factors for the software. This improvement is mainly won through an orderly increase in the level of inspection that the code undergoes. It is also due to an improvement in monitored testing to beyond mere functional parameters.

With this simple certification process in mind I was able to confirm that Forth could indeed be used in the most safety critical projects where a software based solution was a viable choice.

Paul E. Bennett

Paul E. Bennett is an Independent Consultant currently working in the Nuclear Power Industry. He has had experience in many Safety Critical sectors including Petrochemical, Marine, Railway, Medical and Transportation Industries. He has been an advocate of the use Forth in High Integrity Distributed Embedded Control Systems. He has written articles on many topics in Forthwrite including real-world interfacing (see http://www.amleth.demon.co.uk) and www.hidecs.co.uk.

18 – List of Links

Forth Group Germany – www.forth-ev.de

Forth Facebook Group –
https://www.facebook.com/groups/PROGRAMMINGFORTH/

Forth Group – http://www.forth.org/

Silicon Valley Forth – http://www.forth.org/svfig/

Forth Software supplier – www.mpeforth.com
Forth Software supplier – www.Forth.com

Free Mecrisp Forth – http://mecrisp.sourceforge.net/
Free AM Forth – http://amforth.sourceforge.net/
Free 4e4th – http://www.somersetweb.com/4E4th/EN.html
Free noFORTH – http://home.hccnet.nl/anij/nof/noforth.html

My Forth Bookshelf – https://www.amazon.co.uk/Juergen-
Pintaske/e/B00N8HVEZM

Ting's Forth Bookshelf – https://wiki.forth-
ev.de/doku.php/projects:ting_s_electronic_forth_bookshelf

easyFORTH Javascript – https://skilldrick.github.io/easyforth/

19 – Appendix

The Forth Standard – https://forth-standard.org/

Meet Forth Fellows – https://forth-standard.org/users

… Space to add some of your own links here

####

Note: Intentionally left blank

Made in the USA
Middletown, DE
04 August 2018